MISSIONS WITHIN REACH

Intercultural Ministries in Canada

A COMPENDIUM VOLUME OF THE INTERCULTURAL MINISTRIES NATIONAL CONFERENCE OF CANADA, 1993

Enoch Wan, Editor

Missions Within Reach

Editor	: Enoch Wan
Publisher	: China Alliance Press P. O. Box 72289, Kowloon Central Post Office, Hong Kong Tel: (852) 2782 0055 Fax: (852) 2782 0108
North America Distributor	: China Alliance Press (Canada) Inc., 4180-93 Street, Edmonton, Alberta, Canada T6E 5P5 Tel: (403) 463-2002 Fax: (403) 434-7685
Printer	: Sun Light Printing & Bookbinding Factory

First edition, September 1995 2M

ISBN: 962-244-452-0 Cat. No. 4379E

Acknowledgment:
Funding for the printing:
Ruby Johnston Endowment Fund, Regina, Saskatchewan, Canada

TABLE OF CONTENTS

EDITOR

Dr. Enoch Wan
Former Founding Director,
Centre for Intercultural Studies,
Canadian Theological Seminary,
Regina, SK., Canada

Professor of Missions & Anthropology
Director, Doctor of Missiology Program
Reformed Theological Seminary
Jackson, Mississippi, U.S.A.

CONTRIBUTORS

Rev. Denzil Baker
Pastor,
International Friendship Church,
Calgary, Alberta

Dr. Ken Birch
Executive Director,
Home Missions and Bible Colleges,
Pentecostal Assemblies of Canada,
Mississauga, Ontario

Rev. Eliezer Catanus
Pastor, First Baptist Church,
Toronto, Ontario

Dr. Samuel Escobar
Professor of Missiology,
Eastern Baptist Theological Seminary,
Philadelphia, PA.

Rev. Wencesloa Garcia
Programme Coordinator,
World Vision Resettlement Centre,
Mississauga, Ontario

Rev. Ralph Glagau
Pastor, Humberlea Church of God,
Woodbridge, Ontario

Dr. Ross Maracle
President,
National Native Bible College,
Deseronto, Ontario

Dr. Don Moore
Executive Director,
Vision 2000 Canada

Mrs. Marjorie Osborne
Church Growth Coordinator,
Church of the Nazarene Canada

Rev. Eusebio Perez
Pastor, Iglesia Evangelica Hispana,
Toronto, Ontario
National Coordinator for the Spanish Languages
Churches of the Pentecostal Assemblies of Canada.

Rev. Don Posterski
Vice-President of National Programs,
World Vision Canada.

Dr. Alan Roxburgh
Former Director, Centre for Mission
& Evangelism, McMaster University,
Hamilton, Ontario
Senior Pastor, Vancouver Baptist Church, Vancouver, B.C., Canada

Mr. Brian Seim
Director, Canadian Ministries,
International Teams of Canada,
Mississauga, Ontario

Dr. Brian Stiller
Executive Director,
Evangelical Fellowship of Canada

Dr. T.V. Thomas
Director, Centre for Evangelism
& World Mission and
International Minister-at-large,
Every Home International / Canada

Dr. Thomas Wang
Chairman, AD 2000 & Beyond Movement
President, Great Commission Centre, Texas

FOREWORD

Brian Stiller
Executive Director, Evangelical Fellowship of Canada

In the early 1990's in Canada, there was a popular but erroneous story which circulated among evangelicals. It was that the United Nations had declared that Canada was no longer considered Christian. We checked this out with the United Nations both in Canada and New York and found they had never made such a statement. In our research we learned that it had started by a Canadian evangelist who said it in a message. From there it developed a life of its own.

But the story presses one to ask why such a myth would receive such play and acceptance, especially during a time when Canadian social scientists were showing such a surprisingly high level of faith among Canadians.

For the past few years, the Angus Reid Group has been examining what Canadians believe. In 1993 their studies appeared on Maclean's magazine with the rather unbelievable heading (unbelievable in that it was on the cover!) "God Is Alive: Canada is a nation of believers."

Here are some results: 78% of Canadians affiliate with a Christian denomination; 67% believe that "Jesus Christ was crucified, died and was buried but was resurrected to eternal life"; 66% believe that "Christ was the divine son of God"; 62% "believe that the life, death and resurrection of Jesus Christ provided a way for their forgiveness"; 49% "believe that God always answers their prayers."

The point here, of course, is that just because people say they believe does not mean they have made the connection between their brain and their heart and have come to a life-changing encounter with Jesus.

But with these figures--and apart from our propensity to spread rumors--why did this rumor strike a chord among Canadian Christians? Because it sounded as if it could be true. Even though Canada by any societal measurement would be seen by a sociologist as being Christian, we know at the heart of our country there is a deep spiritual malaise.

Recent historical scholarship points out the enormous influence the evangelical Protestant church has had in shaping our country. This influence continued into the mid part of the twentieth century. Within a few decades two realities have become apparent. The radical nature of secularism has pushed faith from having a place in the public life of Canada.

The withdrawal of Bible-believing Christians from leadership in the public square is the second reality. For much of this century we have not been concerned in having a place in helping to format our laws, policies and values.

Now we are at a new moment in which our country is being influenced by new patterns of ethnic and social migration. Within these new patterns we see evidence of hope and possibilities.

My experience has led me to conclude that the secularizing of Canada has not been at the hand of post-1960 immigrants but by those out of European extraction who have been here for decades if not longer. The agenda of stripping the public square of its religious faith and values is not coming by way of the more recent immigrants. Rather they are the ones who seem to stand and affirm the need that Canada retain its religious and Christian base. They are ones who tell me that it has been the Christian heritage which has given to this country the freedoms and values which they as recent immigrants find attractive and cherish.

Now we find the energetic pulse of evangelization coming from intercultural ministries.

I praise God for the vitality they bring to us all. Their vision for outreach and conversion is just what a tired Christian community in Canada needs.

You will find in these pages a stirring challenge for Canadian Christians to see the working of God in this land.

PREFACE

Enoch Wan

Canada welcomes tens of legal immigrants from around the world every single day. Cultural, ethnic and racial diversity is increasingly becoming a significant strand of the national fabric of Canadian society. What is the response of Canadian Christians to this great outreach opportunity provided by this influx of new Canadians? Now that our mission field has moved into our neighborhood, what can we do? Do we Christians, in countries like Canada and the United States of America, realize that **Missions Within Reach** is a true statement in terms of geography, opportunity, viability and reality?

How hard have we tried over the years to evangelize these unreached people who were beyond our reach prior to their immigration from closed countries? Are we aware of the readiness and the receptivity of these new comers to our land due to their psychological state of being up-rooted from the old way into a strange and new environment? Do we realize that their predisposition to the Gospel is also due to their experience of rapid and drastic socio-cultural changes of our time? Are we akin to the ministry of the Holy Spirit whose wooing and moving in their hearts has made them receptive to the Gospel in the midst of their search for meaning, identity and security?

In many ways, **Missions Within Reach** was a unique event that occurred in late September, 1993. It was an **unprecedented** national conference on intercultural ministries in Canada. It was **interdenominational** in scope with more than 100 representatives coming from more than 30 evangelical denominations and para-church organizations. It was **endorsed** by the Evangelical Fellowship of Canada, Vision 2000 Canada and was **co-sponsored** by several dozens of evangelical ministerial agencies. There was **a good mix of Caucasian** and **non-Caucasian** plenary speakers and workshop leaders. It was a catalyst for strategizing and networking for this type of needed outreach ministry. Furthermore, it was held **in Toronto**, the most cosmopolitan city of the world as of 1995.

During the conference there was a **spirit of unity** and a **sense of urgency.** The spontaneous response to the **moving of God's Spirit** and the **movement of God's people** in a concerted effort to pray and cooperate was evident as shown in the **Conference Affirmation**. From the statement of the Affirmation, one can see that the conference objectives as listed below have been achieved:

1. *To motivate and challenge Canadian Christians to engage in intercultural ministries in response to the current demographic trends in Canada;*
2. *To provide leaders and workers of various para-church organizations and denominations a forum for interaction and networking at a national level;*
3. *To create awareness of effective strategies and models of intercultural ministries.*

Towards the end of the conference, participants had expressed the desire to have the plenary sessions and the workshop presentations put in print as a means to carry on the momentum of this spontaneous **Missions Within Reach** movement, a tool to share with others the vision of the conference participants, and a helpful reference for ethnic outreach. All the conference personnel agreed to contribute time and efforts to make the publication of this volume possible. At the closing ceremony, after the public reading of the **Conference Affirmation**, many prayed for the continuation and cooperation in our shared **Missions Within Reach.**

MISSIONS WITHIN REACH CONFERENCE AFFIRMATION

We the participants, both Caucasian and non-Caucasian, attending the first national ***Missions Within Reach*** Conference held in Toronto, September 24-25, 1993, thank God for this conference.

Through our time together, we have celebrated our unity in Christ in the midst of our cultural diversity. We have been refreshed by meeting with people facing the same joys and struggles in ministry. We have developed an increased understanding of the changing social picture in Canada, the biblical basis for inter-cultural ministries, and the value of cooperative efforts in fulfilling Christ's missionary mandate within our nation.

We affirm the many and varied efforts of those who are presently engaged in inter-cultural ministries strategically in evangelism, discipleship, church planting and a testimony to our nation.

We recognize the need for research that would provide a more complete picture of the initiatives and possibilities that God placed before us.

To that end, we would recommend that the impetus of this event be fostered and enhanced for a more complete obedience to Christ's call to make disciples of all peoples and nations to the glory of God.

Toronto, Ontario
September 25, 1993

Chapter 1

MINISTRY IN THE CANADIAN CONTEXT: The Major Markers in the Dominant Culture

---

Don Posterski

Introduction

Last week at the World Vision office, I watched and listened to visitors from Africa. James, black and a native of Kenya was the more passionate and visionary of the two people present. He was optimistic and enthusiastic about the future. He crafted a case for Africa "as the continent of the 21st century."

John was white. A native of South Africa. He was more reflective, more cautious and more calculating than James.

From the side of the room where I was sitting, I had close-up view of the two of them. They were framed in a single picture. One black. The other white. They were not only positional partners in an organization with a mission. They really needed each other. And they were committed to each other.

James and John provide an image of the gospel for us. They are different in temperament, gift and skin colour, but working together on level ground, equal in commitment to the mission of Christ. They portray the best of the future.

My assignment at this conference is specific. The task is to focus on the Canadian cultural frame that cradles all our ministry in Canada.

Accordingly, let's give our attention to: "MINISTRY IN THE CANADIAN CONTEXT: The Major Markers in the Dominant Culture."

Appreciate Canada's Religious Roots and Remaining Privatized Faith -- but Lament the Poverty of the Nation's Collective Spiritual Life

The religious demographics as spelled out by the 1991 Statistics Canada census data map the scene for us. Several aspects of the statistics deserve clarification.

Table 1 - CANADIAN RELIGIOUS AFFILIATION

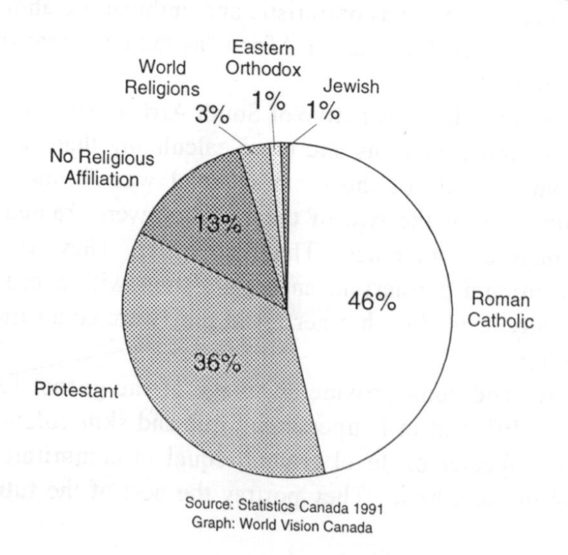

Source: Statistics Canada 1991
Graph: World Vision Canada

In 1971, when 90% of Canadians had European roots, by government decree, Canada formally became a multi-cultural nation.

In 1991, even though we are visually multi-cultural, only 3% of the population identify with other world religions.

Reflecting the secularization of Canadian culture, the largest increase is in the "no religion" category. Whereas only 1% claimed to have "no religion" in 1971, the level increased to 13% in 1991. Still, there is very little anti-Christian sentiment in the culture. By numerical count, out of 27 million people only 21,970 claim to be agnostics and just 13,510 self-identify as atheists.

A total of 82% of Canadians still identify themselves as Christians (46% Catholic and 36% Protestant). The vast majority of Canadians are still "religious something."

However, when it comes to church participation, only 25% attend on any regular basis. Disenchantment with organized religion has already led to disengagement from religious structures for most Canadians. They are constructing their lives without an active role for God. They are like people carrying around expired American Express cards in their wallets. They have a touch of religious status with very little meaning. . .

In his book, "Foolishness to the Greeks", Lesslie Newbigin rightly reminds us that the norms of current Western culture -- which he labels "paganism" -- have been born "out of rejection of Christianity, and are far more resistant to the gospel than the pre-Christian paganism with which cross-cultural missions have been more familiar to them."

Still, if we ignore Canada's religious roots, we will misread the culture to our own peril.

Release Majoritarian Assumptions -- Pursue Principled Pluralism

In the past, our cultural consensus was clearly framed around Judeo-Christian assumptions. Modern Canada is constructed out of the building materials of secular pluralism.

Multi-mindedness characterizes the age. We are not just a multi-cultural society, we are a multi-faith, multi-moral, multi-family structure, multi-gender role, multi-sexual orientation culture. Pervasive multi-mindedness is the forum in which we live -- the place where we need to develop a principled pluralism.

We have a responsibility to influence the culture for God and collective good but, in the 1990's, committed Christians are a cultural minority with more historical status than present cultural influence.

Accept the Demotion of the Pulpit -- Compute the Power of Television

A symbol of the cultural power shift is found in the demotion of the influence of the pulpits of the land and the ascension of the power of television.

In his book, "Out of Control: Global Turmoil on the Eve of the 21st Century," Brzezinski contends that "TV is the most important instrument both for socialization and education" (p.70).

The influence of TV is damaging to our religious cause and tends to erode our cherished cultural values. In the main, TV portrays life without a place or need for God. The July 1993 USA Today states that only 5% of TV characters practice religion in any way and that as a central theme, there is a joke about sex every 4 minutes.

For the church to compete with television will be a miscalculation -- to ignore the medium will be regrettable.

We desperately need committed and gifted Christians to work professionally in the media and television world.

Concede to American Influence -- Assert Canadian Distinctiveness

Canada is profoundly influenced by our southern neighbours but we are not the same. For example, Canada is more pluralistic. A recent example revolves around the issue of gays in the military. In the US, the controversy curtailed presidential power. In Canada, the gays in the military issue provided an afternoon news ripple that got buried on the third page of most newspapers.

Any initiative in Canada that takes away choice or attempts to limit the human rights (especially if the cause targets a minority) will lose.

As evangelicals continue to make gains, it will be a mistake to favor God's blessing with any sense of triumphalism. It will be tragic if we become exclusive and start thinking that we are "all right" and others are "all wrong."

We will continue to be effective as we continue to discern how to INFLUENCE THE CANADIAN WAY.

Relinquish a Soul Cure Gospel -- Affirm a Holistic Gospel

If we could gather up all the prayer letters that have been sent out over the past 25 years and lay them alongside all the organizational appeals for money and then count the number of reported conversions, there would be very few Canadians left to be saved. Something has gone wrong.

Who would argue with the claim that mechanistic evangelism has run out of steam? Words left to stand on their own are weak. Promises of instant transformation combined with dehumanizing methods translate into an unbelievable gospel. Reducing the gospel down to "pray a little prayer for me" conversions is simply not an adequate portrayal of the faith in these times.

Empathetic evangelism has future promise. Evangelism that takes people seriously and responds to the depths of their spiritual needs will gain a hearing. The promises embodied in the substance of a holistic gospel will be a believable gospel.

Beware of Institutional Cynicism -- Strategize for Relational Influence

We are living in a period of institutional cynicism. People do not believe that government, bureaucracies and institutions will be able to provide answers to today's problems. Accordingly, if the church relies on organizational strategies alone, the trend lines will head toward decline.

In the current milieu, establishing personal credibility will be easier and faster than seeking to re-establish institutional credibility.

As the church channels some of its resources and vision into people who go to church but then live in the world, the future will be more promising.

Affirm our Multi-cultural Theory -- Assess Canadian Tolerance for Diversity

According to a recent Angus Reid poll, Canadian's tolerance toward immigration and creating a multi-ethnic culture is under pressure. Using a "tolerance index" the data show that 1/3 are highly tolerant, 1/3 are moderately tolerant and 1/3 are highly/moderately intolerant.

The weight is over toward tolerance and that is especially so for those Canadians who are younger and more highly educated. However, 1 out of 3 people feels that Canada is changing too fast, 1 out of 2 thinks the immigration gate is open too wide and the majority of Canadians urge minorities to become more like other Canadians (whatever that means). We also know that compassion for refugees has also declined.

Clearly, the church has a positive role to play in the construction of Canada's future.

Acknowledge our Historic Importing of Religion -- Contextualize for the Emerging Urban/Global Reality

With the exception of the spirituality of our aboriginal peoples, immigration has always been the primary source of Canada's religious life. In the beginning, people coming from Britain and France defined Canada as Protestant and Catholic.

Today, Canada's immigrant population (those born outside Canada but living legally in the country) totals 4.3 million people or 16% of the population.

The immigration shift from our European heritage to an Asian heritage in the past 25 years is re-defining Canada but maybe not as much as one might assume.

1960's -- 87% of immigration from Europe
3% from Asia
7% from US
3% from Caribbean, Africa & Oceania

1980's -- 43% from Asia
29% from Europe
21% from Caribbean, Africa & Oceania

In understanding the religious make-up of the immigrant population, it is important to remember that Christianity is still the most numerically dominant religion in the world.

According to Roger Nosthakken from the Lutheran Seminary in Saskatoon, a "global village of 1000 people in the 1990's consists of --

329 Christians
174 Muslims
131 Hindus
61 Buddhists
52 Animists
3 Jews
34 from other religions
216 without any religious identification"

The past 150 years of Christian missionary endeavour has been enormously significant. In Canada's case, it means that according to the 1991 census, the immigrant population is 37% Catholic and 30% Protestant. (Compared to the

Canadian born population which is 47% Catholic and 38% Protestant).

Is it any wonder that today in the Toronto area there are at least 60 Korean congregations for their population of 35,000 and at least 110 Chinese congregations for their population of 300,000? The spiritual energy that immigrant Canadians bring to their faith and their commitment to mission and evangelism could be the salvation of the Canadian church.

Chapter 2

BIBLICAL BASIS FOR INTERCULTURAL MINISTRIES: A LATINO PERSPECTIVE

Samuel Escobar

Introduction

As I approach this subject I am very conscious that I write as a very privileged Hispanic Latino. Actually I am a Latin American that came to North America as an adult, a person who had graduated from a university abroad. I did not enter through the hard and dangerous way that the majority of newly arrived Hispanics come. I did not have to suffer through school and society as a "minority" person has to suffer in some parts of North America. At school in Peru I had to suffer some disadvantages as a member of a religious minority in a predominantly Roman Catholic society. But that was nothing compared with the agonies of search for identity, self-rejection and pains of transition that those children and youth of the ethnic minority called Hispanic North American have to endure. Language, Latino culture and our common faith in Jesus Christ have made me aware of the specific needs, problems and dilemmas faced by Latinos in North America, and I have tried to identify with them, trying to do my small part as a teacher, a preacher and a mentor. I am aware that my personal reference might have some bearing on choice of biblical and theological themes for this exposition.

The New Missionary Situation in the World

A fact of our time must be taken as the general frame for any kind of missiological reflection. As we look at the world today we see a marked contrast between the situation at the beginning of this century and the present situation. Andrew Walls has described it saying that "within the last century there has been a massive southward shift of the center of gravity of the Christian world, so that the representative Christian lands now appear to be in Latin America, Sub-Saharan Africa, and other parts of the southern continents" (Walls 1983:226). If the present patterns of church growth and church decline follow the trends of the last three or four decades the picture described by Walls will show even more contrasts as we move into the next millennium. We are witnessing what Walbert Buhlman calls "the coming of the Third Church". He describes it pointing to the fact that the first thousand years of Church history were under the aegis of the Eastern Church in the Eastern part of the Roman empire. In the second millennium the leading Church was the western Church, in the Western part of what used to be the Empire. Then he adds: "Now the Third Millennium will evidently stand under the leadership of the Third Church, the Southern Church. I am convinced that the most important drives and inspirations for the whole church in the future will come from the Third Church" (Buhlman 1986: 6).

Mission scholars are also pointing to another fact of our time. While many non-Western cultures are very receptive to the Gospel of Jesus Christ, paradoxically it is within the Western culture that we find less receptivity to the Gospel. Lesslie Newbigin who was a missionary in India and later returned home to work among the working class people in England says: "the most widespread, powerful, and persuasive among contemporary cultures...modern Western culture...more than almost any other is proving resistant to the Gospel" (Newbigin 1986: 3). There is a kind of reproduction of this picture in North America today. Several of the old mainline denominations show patterns of decline and fatigue with significant numerical losses, while the ethnic churches are growing vigorously. In my own denomination, Anglo churches are declining while Latino, Chinese, Vietnamese and African American congregations are flourishing. It becomes more evident that mission in North America itself will be demanding new patterns of partnership for which the New Testament may have better insights than traditional missiology.

Some crisis for mission in our times and in the coming decades are consequences of this new situation. Anyone interested in obedience to the missionary imperative of the Gospel realizes that to the degree that imperial patterns of mission become obsolete, the New Testament pattern for mission has a renewed relevance for our times. The question is not to make more efficient the missionary practices inherited from the old colonial days, but to revise missionary practices in light of God's Word. One of the best contributions of movements such as the Lausanne movement is precisely that they have called attention to the need to put together missionary zeal and evangelical theology with the kind of historical awareness and cultural sensitivity that the hour demands. Missionary awareness today requires a realistic grasp of a threefold challenge: mission to the West, mission to the un-reached elsewhere, mission at our doorstep. Within the frame of this new awareness I want to explore the biblical basis for an inter-cultural missionary effort.

The Scope of God's Salvation is Universal

Through the pages of Scripture runs the self-revelations of God that wants to bless all human beings because he loves his whole creation and wants to save every human being. The compassion of God is the note that marks the teaching of the prophets and without it we cannot understand the existence of Israel nor the mission of Jesus Christ. But through the pages of Scripture runs also the story of a tension within the people of God. A tension between the very meaning of their missionary existence to be a blessing to all nations and all peoples, and at the same time the temptation to selfishly enjoy of the blessings of their privileged position and to be disobedient to God.

Luke describes this tension both in his Gospel as well as in the Book of Acts. Thus, for instance, the strong denunciation of Jesus in the parable of the barren fig tree (Luke 13: 1-9) comes as the culmination of a mounting tension between the established religion of Israel and Jesus, the fulfillment of the prophetic promises, who is rejected by the most devout people. The rejection of salvation for the Gentiles in the synagogue of Pysidian Antioch (Acts chapter 13, especially vv,42-52) is another instance of that tension. In view of the resistance of the Jewish believers, Paul takes upon himself the obedience to the missionary purpose of God using the statement from Isaiah as a paradigm: "I have appointed you to be a light to the gentiles, and a means of salvation to the earth's farthest bounds" (Acts 13: 47 NEB). Keep in mind that culture plays an important part in this tension. Even within the church of Jerusalem it is evident that contact with those who are different is an act intolerable to the Jews. They reproached Peter for "visiting men who are uncircumcised" as well as "sitting at table with them" (Acts 11:1-4).

The Church Embodies Universality

There is a way in which a good part of the New Testament material can be read as the description of the crisis provoked by the first steps towards the internationalization of mission, and the Apostolic answer to it. As the Gospel moves from the Jewish world into the Gentile world, missionary responsibility passes from the homogeneous first generation of Jewish believers to the heterogeneous communities in the Greco-Roman world. The Apostle Paul was chosen by God as the champion of this great missionary step which has a paradigmatic value for the Church through the ages. I believe that Luke's writings reflect Paul's convictions and that other writings like those of John show other dimensions of the same development.

In order to formulate the response of the Church, I think it is important to remember that in the biblical vision of reality there are some elements that are unique, that cannot be pushed into the mold of contemporary worldviews, and that as Yoder has said "stand in creative tension with the cultural functions of our age or perhaps of any age" (Yoder 1972: 5). The Church is the community that lives by the biblical vision. The Church proclaims that the existence of the universe and human history can only be understood and make sense within the purpose of God, manifested in Jesus Christ by the power of the Holy Spirit. Rene Padilla has expressed it eloquently, "With the coming of Jesus Christ, all barriers that divide humankind have been broken down and a new humanity is now taking shape in and through the Church" (Padilla 1985: 142). Because the church sees her own existence as the fulfillment of that biblical vision and lives by it, she is therefore a community which embodies that creative tension with all the contradictions and agonies that it involves.

The life of the Church must be an embodiment of the message she proclaims. A new kind of life that will be a contrast with the prejudices and discriminations predominant in society is the direct result of the kind of message the Church proclaims. As Padilla says, "The salvation that the Gospel proclaims is not limited to man's reconciliation to God. It involves the remaking of man in all the dimensions of his existence. It has to do with the recovery of the whole man according to God's original purpose for his creation (Padilla 1985: 79). As a missionary community set in the midst of historical processes the church can only accomplish her mission by being "in the world", through the instrumentality of the cultural elements that surround her.

As she goes about the fulfillment of her mission, the church affects cultural functions, making some of them obsolete, or transforming and redeeming others. The life of the church within each different context even creates new cultural functions in every age. However, when by her own presence and mission the church has contributed to shape a culture, the fatal day comes when she lets herself be pushed into the mold of the age, leaving aside the hardship of creative tension for the comfortable position of total inculturation. In the history of missions, there were transitional periods in which missionaries had rendered the service as the prophetic voice. They stood right at the center of that "creative tension," embodying in their persons the dilemmas and agonies of a life between the times. Hispanic churches are right now in a frontier situation, a society that has to be seen as a mission field.

A key to answer the missionary novelty of the Church in the time of Paul can help us at this point. We must remember that Paul was not writing treatises of systematic theology but answering questions that came from a missionary situation. In the encounter of cultures and races that was the milieu of mission in the first century, Paul's teaching on the new humanity that God was creating had an unique relevance. We must grasp anew the significance of that teaching. Thus in 2 Corinthians, Paul makes the bold and revolutionary statement "From now on we regard no one from a worldly point of view. Though we once regarded Christ in this way we do so no longer. Therefore if anyone is in Christ, he is a new creation! the old has gone the new has come!" (2 Cor. 5: 18-17 NIV).

The "newness" that Paul is proclaiming is closely connected with his own missionary work as a Jewish man who happens to be a missionary to Gentiles. "He does not perceive people as Jew or Greek, but as the new people whom they have become in Christ. Because Christ has taken the place of all, now all persons can be seen in the image of Christ" (Yoder 1970:131). And precisely what Paul is doing is founding churches, communities of new people which are to express the novelty brought by the Gospel. The "newness" cannot be perceived in isolated individual believers. It is perceived in the embrace that has turned hostility into hospitality, by which a Gentile has found Abraham as a father and a Jew has found the Gentile as a brother in Christ. The Apostles were ready to face the complex pastoral problems derived from that condition. Precisely this was the novelty brought by the existence of the Church, a testimony to the transforming power of the Gospel.

Patterns of Missionary Partnership

When we look at the missionary advance in the New Testament material, we also find a most suggestive practice of cooperation and partnership between different churches, within the theological frame we have described. The New

Testament principle, for cooperation and fellowship in mission in a cross-cultural international situation is the principle of reciprocity, and was developed by the Apostle Paul as he tried to explain the financial side of his missionary practice. The passages in Romans 15: 14-33 and 2 Corinthians chapters 8 and 9 are very clear on this. The principle became operative in his famous collection among the Gentile churches of Macedonia and Achaia for the poor in Judea, on the basis that "if the Gentiles have shared in the Jews' spiritual blessings, they owe it to the Jews to share with them their material blessings." (Romans 15:27 NIV). Each one, whether he be a Jew or a Gentile, had made his own contribution to the life of the Church in mission, and it is as if Paul would be putting all contributions on the table in order to establish a pattern of relationship developing from the recognition of the gifts. This pattern could be described with the words mutuality and reciprocity.

Paul's objective, especially in light of Romans 15:14-29, is the promotion of mission. Paul wants to get the believers in Rome involved in his missionary enterprise to Spain: "I hope to visit you while passing through and to have you assist me on my journey there..." (v.24). So he explains that he is now engaged in a very important missionary task of holistic mission even before his apostolic church planting task as a pioneer missionary in Spain. But he also encourages his Roman readers to be involved in mission by pointing out the exemplary generosity of the saints in Macedonia and Achaia. Within that context, he establishes the principle of mutuality and reciprocity. He also uses the example of the Macedonians to challenge the Corinthians (2 Cor. 8:1-7;9: 1-5) and praises the former for doing their part joyfully and sacrificially. Paul highlights the fact that the Macedonians "gave themselves to the Lord and to us," and encourages the Corinthians to "also excel in this grace of giving." For Paul the Corinthians' participation in this aspect of mission is not merely an economic transaction of "supplying the needs of God's people", it has a eucharistic dimension, "men will praise God for the obedience that accompanies your confession of the Gospel of Christ." From this principle I see three important points:

First, there is a recognition of others and their contribution to members within the Body of Christ. It is possible to take Paul's image of the Body (1 Cor. 12) and understand it at an international scale. Another aspect involved is respect for the particular gifts that each one brings to the common cause. No one of them, spiritual or material, is to be presented as better than the other. Both count. A third point is a holistic approach in which both material and spiritual gifts are perceived as concrete realities for the common cause. From this, much could be learned about partnership between ethnic churches and mainline churches.

Equality is another principle at work in the financial relationship established between the Gentile churches and the Jewish church. Paul develops it also within the spiritual context of their mutual belonging to the Body of Christ. "Our desire - argues the Apostle - is not that others may be relieved while you are hard pressed, but that there might be equality. At the present time your plenty will supply what they need so that in turn their plenty will supply what you need. Then there will be equality" (2 Cor. 8: 13-14). It is fascinating to read commentaries about this passage in which North American scholars become terribly defensive about this kind of distributive or egalitarian "socialism" so clearly stated by Paul. I think the best way to understand this truth is in the context of mutuality and reciprocity, and in the context of the Old Testament practice and teaching as alluded by Paul in 2 Cor. 8: 15.

The whole idea of a collection from the Gentile churches for poor Jews in Judea was something completely unusual in those days. Not Jews from the diaspora sending help to Jews in Palestine; but financial help across ethnic and cultural barriers. Therein displays the creativity of Paul's missionary ministry. As usual, he explains his practice in relation to deeper theological truths that are central to the Christian faith. As Minear has said "...as Paul sees it, Christ makes every man a debtor to all those for whom Christ died. He thereby creates a fabric of mutual interdependence... This common debt gives to believers a common mission, whether the debt be honored by welcoming all to table-fellowship, by sharing in a philanthropic contribution, or by supporting the missionary campaign to Spain" (Minear 1971: 104-105). Our times of internationalization of mission or trans-cultural mission within a nation pose many new questions. **Mission Within Reach** in North America, takes place within a complex multi-cultural mosaic, and it involves an array of new pastoral and missiological problems. I think that we will find the answer to some of them in the single but radical novelty of apostolic practice. To grasp it, we must dare to take issue with the presuppositions and the accepted wisdom of our own societies which are far from being Christian. And we must also be creative in developing new partnerships, in obedience to God, within a new missionary situation.

Works Cited

Walbert Buhlman The Church of the Future Orbis, 1986.

Paul Minear The Obedience of Faith SCM Press, 1971.

Lesslie Newbigin Foolishness to the Greeks, The Gospel and Western Culture WCC, Geneva 1986.

C. Rene Padilla Mission Between the Times Eerdmans, 1985.

Andrew Walls "The Gospel as the Prisoner and Liberator of Culture" Evangelical Review of Theology Vol. 7, No. 2, 1983.

John Howard Yoder The Politics of Jesus Eerdmans, 1972.

Chapter 3

MOBILIZING FOR INTERCULTURAL MINISTRIES

T.V. Thomas

It was Wednesday, January 16, 1991. I was in the living room of my home watching the early evening newscast when I heard the then President of the United States, George Bush, declare "The liberation of Kuwait has begun." Before he made that public statement I knew much had been done before Operation Desert Storm became a reality. Much strategic thinking and planning had been done before troops and defence equipment began to land on the sands of the Middle East.

That is the image I have when I look at the word "mobilizing." The dictionary defines it as "to put into action" or "to place in active service". When we talk about Mobilization for Intercultural Ministries what I am referring to is the engagement of a concerted, united, well-planned, enthusiastic and all out effort in reaching the ethnics in Canada.

Why Mobilize?

There are several reasons why there are no options but to mobilize. Two major reasons have already been addressed at this Conference. First, Dr. Samuel Escobar has clearly outlined for us the biblical and theological reasons why the church must be engaged in mission. Secondly, Don Posterski painted the changing landscape of Canada and how it has become ethnically and religiously pluralistic. My dear friends, I want to draw your attention to the fact that there is a color change across Canada. In the last 25 years, Canada has gone from predominantly monochrome to color chrome! Canada's mosaic is emerging more colorful than ever. In some of our larger cities complete city blocks have more ethnics than whites. With so many Chinese from Hong Kong now residing in Vancouver, some in the media have nicknamed it "Hongcouver."

But let me suggest a third reason why we must mobilize. It is because, I believe, these ethnic groups are winnable for Jesus. New environments increase openness to new values. Exposing the claims of Christ to them in their early stages of life in Canada is an efficient approach with possibilities of higher yield in salvation. It is important to note that most of the conversions recorded in the Book of Acts are of individuals who are away from home or place of origin!

What Can Be Done to Mobilize?

What must the Church do to mobilize? What must the Christian do to seize the opportunity? Let me suggest six steps to mobilize for reaching new Canadians.

1. Catch the Vision

Ironically, many in the church including leaders have not caught the vision of what God is doing by bringing ethnic peoples within our evangelistic reach. You can place

Canadian Christians in five categories by the maladies they suffer from.

a. Those who miss it

There are Christians who can physically see the color change but really don't see the vision of reaching ethnics. They suffer from acute color blindness.

b. Those who neglect it

These are Christians who see what is happening in their communities with so many immigrants but refuse to do anything about it. They simply ignore the opportunities. These suffer from a callous heart. They need the compassionate heart of Jesus which goes out to lost people everywhere.

c. Those who put it off

These are those in the body of Christ in Canada who believe something needs to be done but they postpone action. There are other priorities on their missionary agenda. They have every intention to do something without a fixed starting date in the near future of reaching immigrants. These are people who suffer from hyper-procrastination.

d. Those who give up on it

These "give-uppers" see what God is doing all around them only too clearly. Having analyzed the statistics they are aware of the reality of changing neighborhoods with multi-lingual children in schools, ethnic grocery stores and restaurants, colorful wardrobes and styles. They are only too aware of these Canadian realities but they are overwhelmed by them. They suffer from paralysis by over analysis.

e. Those who play with it

These are Christians and Christian agencies who have already started doing something about addressing the evangelism of new Canadians but they are playing with it. These are like the people at the swimming pool who dangle their feet in the water and give the impression that they are swimming. This is the disease of hypocritical tokenism. There are so many who give the impression that they are serious about the vision without embracing the total responsibility.

Praise God that there is a sixth group of people. This group is in stark contrast to those in the other five categories. These Canadian Christians have caught the vision of what God is doing, embraced the opportunities for mission in Canada and are enthusiastically working for it. This is still a small group. They want to cooperate and be fulfillers of the prophecy of what we read in Revelation 7:9-10. *After these things I looked, and behold, a great multitude, which no one could count, from every nation and all tribes and peoples and tongues, standing before the throne and before the Lamb, clothed in white robes, and palm branches were in their hands; and they cry out with a loud voice, saying, "Salvation to our God who sits on the throne, and to the Lamb."*

I believe you are attending this Conference because you are part of this group -- the winning group. I believe a dedicated minority like you can make a difference in your church, your denomination and in your community.

2. Communicate the Vision

Catching the vision is only the initial step in mobilizing. We need to communicate that vision. We need to grassroots this vision to those who have not caught it yet. How do we communicate the vision? The following are suggestions one can try:

a. Through focused prayer.

   I am learning that one of the most effective ways of communicating the vision is through personal prayer. As we begin praying for the spiritually lost among the ethnic groups, God the Holy Spirit will work in us. He will engrave more and more of a passion for this vision.

b. Through sharing this burden as prayer requests in your circles of influence.

   As other people begin to pray for the needs of ethnics, God has ways of getting them involved in intercultural ministries.

c. Through having ethnic pastors speak in your pulpit about their ministries and what God is doing.

d. Through quality media presentations of opportunities for intercultural ministries.

e. Through a visit to a part of the city where there is a large enough concentration of ethnic people, e.g. one ministry started because a pastor took his Board after a Saturday morning prayer meeting on a walking tour of an area of town where a certain ethnic group lived. They caught a vision and a church planting effort began.

3. Realize the Vision

To realize the vision there must be concerted efforts in ethnic evangelism and church planting. At least the following five guidelines need to be followed to be successful:

a. Need to score super high in relational evangelism.

   We are aware of research that has borne out the fact that Canadians generally respond better to the Gospel in the context of relationships rather than just program-based evangelism or institutional flag waving. If that is true with white Canadians in general, it is at least doubly true with non-caucasians. Showing love and care along with building meaningful relationships prepare the receptive soil for the truth of the Gospel to be sown.

b. Need to be aware that the rate of receptivity to the Gospel differs from ethnic group to ethnic group or religious group to religious group.

   Some ethnic groups are more resistant than others. This has been true all through mission history. For instance, working with Muslims brings slower results than working among Filipinos. Most Filipinos have Roman Catholic roots and all that they need in evangelism is to complete the Gospel story with biblical undergirding. For evangelizing most Muslims one needs to help remove barriers before beginning to tell the Gospel story. We need to also remember that Muslims from Indonesia are far more receptive than those from the Middle East. The germination time for the Gospel varies significantly from group to group.

c. Need to begin church planting, small but strong.

I have seen too many false starts in ethnic church planting in North America. But false starts are costly. They are not only costly financially; but more tragically they are costly in personnel. Misunderstanding, frustration, emotional pain, sense of failure are experienced by well-intentioned Christian workers. Some have gone into ethnic church planting with glamour and left with gloom. I have personally met some of them who have left their ministries as emotionally damaged people and feeling they were abused. Their stories are painful to the ear as well as to the heart.

How do we avoid false starts and reduce our losses? Here are some questions that need to be honestly answered prior to the venture:

(1) Have you done research before you begin the work?
(2) Have you analyzed the data well?
(3) Have you developed a working plan?
(4) Have you properly negotiated the terms of reference and working conditions to all involved?
(5) Have you chosen or appointed personnel carefully?

(6) Who supports this ministry with prayers and finances and for how long?

(7) Who is going to encourage and supervise that venture?

d. Need to have a team approach to ministry than solo approaches.

The principle of team ministry is effective in most ministries and particularly true among ethnic evangelism and church planting ventures. Have two or three to form a team. May I remind you that this is not a new idea for the Book of Acts is replete with examples. A team provides a better spiritual gift-mix, mutual support, more wisdom and more encouragement to each other. I believe there is no better way to develop strong future leaders for the church than to work in a team. Even inter-racial teams can be an incredible witness. When they function well it becomes a living demonstration of the reconciling power of the Gospel.

e. Need to present the whole Gospel to the whole person.

There needs to be a high commitment to the holistic gospel. Our approach needs to go beyond being interested just in a person's soul. We must meet the needs of the total person. Let us not fragment the person when God has given us an unfragmented Gospel. This calls for social concern and an encouragement of compassion/mercy ministries.

4. Recruit for the Vision

Evangelism and church planting among ethnic people is one of the latest and most attractive fronts of recruiting personnel for ministry. Where can we recruit them? There are several sources:

Source #1 **Importing from overseas**

In some instances it might be okay to import some church planters from the country of the ethnic group you are targeting. For example many of the first Chinese churches in Canada were planted by Chinese pastors who were recruited from Hong Kong.

I want to warn you that you can import unwisely. There are two problem categories. One is the misfits. The misfits do not cut it culturally or cannot handle ministry in an urban environment.

The other wrong group to be imported are the opportunists. These are those who are willing to come to Canada for wrong motives. They use the system for personal gain -- to gain entrance and to make it rich.

In light of these two factors I want to give two cautions about importing pastors: First, select carefully and select hard. Do not be attracted to someone because they are eager and available. Second, provide adequate and personalized orientation for the pastor and family so that they have a fighting chance at success in establishing their ministry. But let me quickly remind you that importing personnel from overseas is at best a short-gap measure for the short-term.

Source #2 **Overseas Missionaries**

An excellent source are missionaries who have returned to Canada because of family-related or health reasons. Even some who have retired from the mission field but still enjoy good health and would like to remain in active ministry could be a great source. These missionaries already know the language, culture and customs and have the ministry experience.

May I be bold enough to suggest that it may be even wise to strategically and proactively assign some of the seasoned and effective missionaries to pioneer some of the ethnic church planting in Canada. I am increasingly convinced that geographical location should not be the primary criterion of personnel assignment but an unreached people group. For the Japanese in Calgary are as precious to Jesus as those Japanese living anywhere in Japan! The same is true of the Chileans, Filipinos, Haitians, Itureans or any people group in Canada.

Source #3 **Missionary Candidates**

I am flipping the coin here to my previous suggestion. Why can't we assign a missionary candidate who is targeting to work in a Middle Eastern country to work on a ministry team that is reaching out to Arabs in Montreal for a couple of years? Such opportunities for missionary candidates would be wonderful on-the-job training for them to learn the culture and even the language before they land in Beirut or Cairo.

Source #4 **Canadian Grown Leadership**

As the second generation of immigrants are growing and evangelized they can be challenged to consider full-time ministry opportunities. It is encouraging to see the upward trend in attendance of second generation ethnic students at several of the urban ministry training institutions in the country. Again, personal counsel and financial aid would go a long way to encourage them while they struggle with temptations of materialism presented through family and peers.

5. Finance the Vision

I often hear church leaders at the local, district and national levels talk about the lack of funds in initiating or expanding their intercultural ministry efforts.

I find the lack of funds is not as great a problem as a lack of vision; lack of finances is not as great a problem as a lack of courage to change; lack of money is not as great a hindrance as our lack of ability to communicate that vision to the pew. "New money" will emerge when there is "new vision" in our hearts. The giving of resources always follows a vision that is communicated. For I have always said since coming to this continent: God owns the cattle on a thousand hills and the price of beef is going up! If we really mean business in reaching new Canadians, we will have to make a concerted effort in communicating this vision clearly to the Body of Christ. If we are serious about the salvation of the new Canadians then we will even re-allocate some of the funds that we raise for overseas missions. We perhaps have to reeducate our constituencies that we believe in global or world missions and not just overseas missions. Again, the criterion for distribution of funds needs to be focused on an unreached people group rather than geographic distance. I believe funding is not the handicap but owning the vision of the unreached ethnics and communicating it are the problems.

6. Partnership in the Vision

I know partnership is a buzz word in mission circles today. I hope it becomes more than a buzz word. It is my prayer that we will see partnership as a biblical expectation of all Christian believers and as a viable means to maximize our efforts to the cause of Christ.

In the uncertain economic times we live in, partnership will soon become the only sane way to survive. Corporate business has realized this already. Cooperation, strategic alliances and mergers have become the order of the day in the business world.

The rugged individualism coupled with affluence of the West have afforded us the bad habit of not partnering in the Kingdom of God agendas. A study of the In-Depth Evangelism Movement of the 1960's and 70's will surface the fundamental principle that guided its success: "Where Christians pool their resources together God multiplies them." The resources they pooled were not limited to finances but personnel and expertise as well. We as Christians cannot go on with the "business as usual" mindset. Let us be honest and face up to the present realities. We must begin to prayerfully communicate and lay down tracks for partnership.

Some Partnership Possibilities

1. Establishing a Research and Data Base Centre

This centre could map out Canada to track the distribution and movement of ethnic groups. It could be a great resource to Canadian Church if it could provide helpful monographs of unreached people groups. A newsletter of ideas and strategies could be produced by the centre and distributed.

2. Developing Target Group Focus

I think we would be smart enough to cooperate and decide what ethnic group in what location would be the primary focus for a mission agency or denomination. Then each can specialize and develop expertise and resources to reaching certain groups.

3. Equipping Ministry Personnel

A survey of most of the current faculty in most of theological training centers will reveal that they are predominantly Caucasian. Most of them have not developed a cross-cultural framework or even sensitivity. Therefore, the graduates from these theological schools who are interested in inter-cultural ministries need additional training and this could be through partnership.

We need to see partnership in developing non-traditional methods and delivery systems for their training of ethnic leadership. Why can't courses or seminars be jointly sponsored in certain locations? Why can't study conferences be held to wrestle with some aspects of ethnic evangelism? The joint sponsorship of this conference was an incredible example of what can be done for the benefit of all. But this is only a first step of a long road ahead.

4. Developing Ministry Resources

Only through partnership can cassettes, videos and tracts for evangelism be affordably produced. The Canadian Bible

Society needs commendation for providing Bibles in many languages by producing "diaglot" scriptures -- having English and one other language side-by-side.

I believe the need for partnership in the vision of evangelizing new Canadians is no longer a luxury option. It is an indisputable necessity.

Chapter 4

Global Implications of Reaching the New Canadians

Thomas Wang

Introduction

I have been looking forward to this occasion though I recently have a very busy ministry schedule. The title of this plenary session is "Global Implications of Reaching New Canadians." It is exciting to live in our time and in a changing world. The world is going through a period of rapid changes: socially, economically, politically, spiritually, technologically, high mobility, etc.

A Timely Theme

Demographers have been informing us of the high mobility of contemporary society. The mobility in various parts of the world takes different forms: migration to the city in the process of urbanization, migrating for political and economic reasons in the form of immigration. Canada and the United States of America are two of the most desirable countries for immigrants from the Two-Thirds world. Subsequently, we do not have to go overseas in order to be involved in Christian missions. With the influx of immigrants to North America, now we can evangelize people who come from many lands, including countries closed to the Gospel such as communist and Muslim nations. The theme of the conference **Missions Within Reach** is a wonderful choice in several ways.

It is "Missions Within Reach" in terms of the geography and opportunity. It is "Missions Within Reach" in terms of viability and reality. Indeed, it is a **meaningful theme**. It is also a **timely theme** for our target audience is ready and receptive. People nowadays are living in a world of transition. They have experienced war, famine, economic crisis, political unrest, moral decline with the disappearance of absolutes and all these factors are contributing to preparing them for the time-honored Gospel with an unchanging message. Therefore, "Missions Within Reach" is indeed an **excellent theme**. If at all possible, I would like to see it being part of the program or a topic of discussion in the up-coming GCOWE '95 (Global Consultation on World Evangelization) in Seoul, Korea in 1995.

Attitude of Recipient Countries

Historically, there are many countries founded and formed by immigrants. Canada and the United States of America are just two of these immigrant countries. People in the recipient countries can easily be proud and be prejudiced against the new arrivals. What should be their attitude towards new comers?

In the early history of Canada and the United States, the countries were founded by Christian immigrants from the old world with basic Christian values and principles. As evangelicals, let us examine and learn from the history of the nation of Israel in the Old Testament.

Even at the time when Israel was a mobile nation before settling in the promised land of Canaan, they received foreigners who moved into their community and lived among them. The following passages from the Bible are instructively helpful to understand God's expectation of His people's attitude towards the new arrivals residing among them:

Deut . 10:18	- show mercy
Deut . 24:17	- absence of discrimination
Lev. 19:10	- be generous
Lev. 25:6	- equality of provision
Num. 15:15	- equality of personal value and worth
Ex. 23:9	- equality under the law/justice
Num. 9:14	- equality of religion
Num. 35:15	- equality of protection by law
Lev. 24:16	- equality of punishment

These should be the characteristics of all Christian nations and should be the proper attitude evident among the recipient countries in their dealing with new immigrants.

I personally have experienced the evident kindness of Americans shown towards me as an immigrant from China decades ago. There were many incidents during my early years of adjusting to the American culture while attempting to evangelize American citizens and residents. Even non-Christians showed me their kindness, hospitality and generosity. When I came with no English language skills, no relative or friend in this strange land, God used Christian and non-Christian Americans to help me.

Years later, when I had established myself in ministry, I became involved in many forms of ministry and travelled extensively to many lands. I came to realize that the kindness of Americans towards immigrants is not commonly found in many parts of the world.

There is a general notion that immigrants are all alike. That is not true. Among those coming to North America are immigrants of great variety and complexity. Let me illustrate from the ethnic group I know best which is the Chinese in North America. They include categories such as:

ABC	American-born Chinese
CBC	Canadian-born Chinese
MIT	Made-in-Taiwan
IFHK	Imported from Hong King
OBC	Overseas-born Chinese

They immigrated to North America with different motivations: economic, political, etc. They came in different ways. For example, the manual laborers took a four-month long journey by steam ship from China decades ago. In the 1970's, refugees of Chinese descent from Vietnam came as boat-people. Recently there is the influx of affluent merchants flying first-class from Hong Kong before the critical year of 1997. Then there are the ABC/CBC born of immigrant parents whose mother tongues are: Cantonese, Mandarin, English, etc. When looking at their level of education, you will find the unschooled farmers who are illiterate both in Chinese and English as compared to the university professors/researchers in prestigious American institutions. The degree of assimilation of the OBC from the country-side of China differs from those who come from the Portuguese colony of Macau. Then there are the thoroughly westernized ABC/CBC who are Chinese in appearance but Americans/Canadians in essence.

As you can see, new comers to North America have different needs, with diverse backgrounds and varied aspirations. Whoever they may be, we should show Christian kindness towards them, in a Christ-like manner to live among them, with God-glorifying witness befriending them and a fruitful ministry to win them over for the Gospel.

Attitude of New Comers

People may differ in the "why," "when" and "how" when immigrating to North America. Since they choose to come to the country of their choice, they should make the necessary adjustment in the new environment. I will selectively mention several basic principles regarding the proper attitude of these new comers in their adopted country.

New immigrants should **enjoy** what is established by the "blood" of the founding fathers. Both in Canada and the United States, the early immigrants in the new world had to struggle for survival. They fought battles and shed blood to gain independence from colonial governments of Europe. They suffered hardship to form and found the immigrant nations. They labored and toiled to develop and improve life and living condition for several centuries. New comers should be **grateful** for the rich heritage and abundant resources passed down from the forefathers to them. They should be **respectful** to the history, the tradition and the order of the land.

Again let me illustrate from personal experience and long-time observation among the Chinese. For hundreds of years Chinese have been immigrating to many countries, especially in Southeast Asia. They settled down in countries like Malaysia, Singapore, Indonesia, the Philippines, etc. and had prospered materially and financially. However, many of them had received kind assistance from the local people of different societies; yet they gave very little in return. For generations, they thought only of themselves and had been very slow in reciprocating to their generous hosts. With accumulated wealth and acquired influence they **demanded respect** from nationals. No wonder from time to time, and from place to place, there have been strong anti-Chinese riots and legislations with physical violence and government edicts to expel them from theses countries.

In the newly adopted state, new comers should **not take things for granted**. They should **not demand respect** from those who have come before them and have given much to assist them. New comers in these immigrant countries should **contribute their share and conduct themselves as good citizens**. All the more, if he is a Christian he is required by the Scripture to do so. **Respect is earned and cannot be legislated.** There is no room for new comers, either by attitude or action, to bring about "reverse discrimination" in a multi-ethnic and multi-cultural society.

In immigrant nations, with democratic governments such as Canada and the United States of America, there are checks and balances, democracy and harmony, freedom and equality, pluralism and tolerance. How would you answer this question: "Is God tolerant?" The answer is both "yes" and "no". God is tolerant in that He provides rain and sunshine to both the just and the unjust by His common grace (Mt 5:45). He loves the world and desires all to be saved. Yet He is absolutely holy and righteous without compromise. He loves sinners but will not tolerate sin. Similarly, our toleration has limits beyond which we cannot go without minimizing God's revelation and compromising our commitment to Him. We have to recognize that there is a demarcation line over which we cannot pass. We do not approve or condone sin; yet we are to tolerate and co-exist with sinners. For example, we are to accept Muslims as they are but cannot condone their practice of polygamy.

Temporarily, during our pilgrimage in life on this earth, we live among non-Christians to be salt and light (Mt 5:13-16). Regardless of the new immigrants' place of origin or choice of religion, we are to love them, share the life of Christ and the love of God with them - praying that the love and the life of God will touch them through us.

Conclusion

We are living in a changing world which is characterized by high mobility (including immigration), moral relativity (including the disappearance of the absolutes), and religious and ethnic plurality (including people of different ethnic origins and religious affiliations) living together in a multi-ethnic and multi-cultural society.

We Christians, living in such a multi-religious and multi-ethnic context, have discovered that there is **Missions Within Reach** in our neighborhood. There are people with all kinds of need: spiritual, physical, emotional, etc. We must not be overwhelmed by horizontal needs at the expense of the vertical reality. We are the Church.

The Church is God's mouthpiece like the prophet of old and the "lamp stand" made of gold. We are to speak the truth and are to practice it too. As members of the Church whether we are new immigrants or long-time residents, all have both vertical and horizontal responsibilities. We are both citizens of the City of God and the city of temporal residence. Whichever country we find ourselves in, we have a duty to **keep the nation under God**.

We are to **be aware** of the evangelistic opportunities around us for we live in immigrant countries within a multi-religious context. We are to **be selective** in the choice of evangelistic approaches appropriate to the recipients of the

Gospel. We are to be **careful**, not to destroy the moral and ethical nature of recipient Christian nations. We must do everything we can to **keep the nation under God** for new comers can pollute, as did Queen Jezebel during the time of king Ahab leading the nation into Baal worship (I Kings 18).

There are many tangible ways we could influence key-people to **keep the nation under God**. Being an American citizen, every year I write letters to top political leaders of the United States of America. Recently, I just sent out eight hundred letters to elected officials in Congress, the Governors, the President and members of his cabinet. I have called them to pray and seek God's face. We are to be active and be encouraged for ours is the God-given mandate to be involved in **Missions Within Reach** in both theory and practice.

Chapter 5

REACHING THE UNREACHED PEOPLE GROUPS OF SOUTH ASIA IN CANADA

DENZIL R. BAKER

Understanding the Diversity Among South Asians

The term "South Asians" in the context of cross-cultural evangelism is misleading. It gives the impression that we are dealing with one homogeneous unit. In fact, the people represented in this geographical area are very diverse. This becomes clear when we consider the history, culture, religions and languages of the countries listed in this region; namely India, Pakistan, Nepal, Bangladesh, Sri Lanka and the Maldives (see **MAP 1** below).

Map 1 - SOUTH ASIA

India which makes up 3/4 of the population of South Asia is itself extremely diverse. While 85% of its population are Hindus, it represents many different brands of Hinduism with hundreds of deities. Popular Hinduism differs from philosophical Hinduism. Ten percent of India's population are Muslims, composed of Sunni, Shiite and some branches of Shiite Islam. India also has Christians of various denominations and also Buddhists, Sikhs and Jains.

Culturally, India is as diverse as it is religiously. Each of the seventeen provinces has its own main language and distinct culture.

A study of the other six countries will demonstrate the same level of diversity, with Islam, Buddhism and Hinduism being the predominant religions.

While there are some broad similarities, each country has its own distinct culture, history and national sense of pride, with obvious differences within any one country, as we have seen in the case of India.

So the people coming to Canada from South Asia are very diverse, each bringing with them strong cultural, religious and family ties from their home country. Each one also comes with their own personal history.

Table 1 - MAJOR SOURCE COUNTRIES

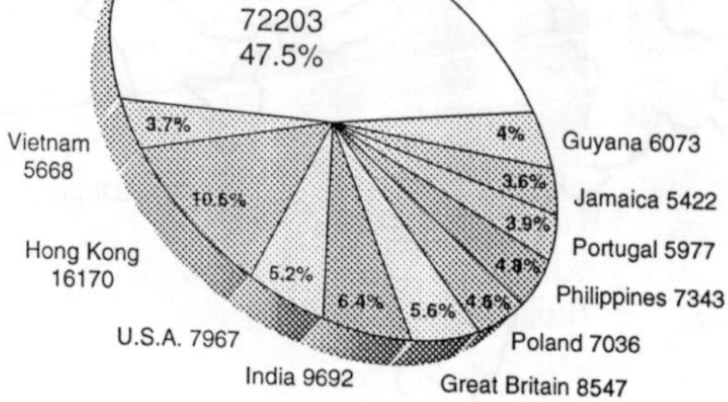

OTHER 72203 47.5%
Vietnam 5668
Hong Kong 16170
U.S.A. 7967
India 9692
Great Britain 8547
Poland 7036
Philippines 7343
Portugal 5977
Jamaica 5422
Guyana 6073

Table 1 shows that South Asia provides the second highest number of immigrants coming to Canada. India alone provides 6.4% while the other six countries are counted in the category "others".

Table 2 below gives us an idea as to where the immigrants are distributed. The concentration is in our major cities.

Table 2 - SOUTH ASIANS IMMIGRATING TO CANADA

(By Major Cities)

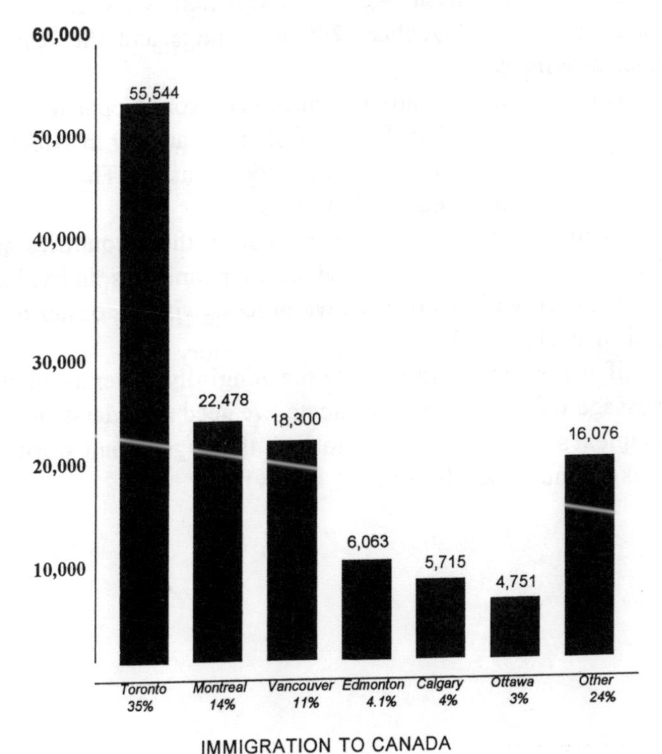

IMMIGRATION TO CANADA
1988

The total Asian population in Canada as of 1991 is 228,794. The national total of people listing under "India" in terms of "place of origin" is 173,675: with 88,450 living in Ontario; 52,680 in British Columbia; 15,285 in Alberta and the rest in other provinces.

There are 25,440 immigrants in Canada from Sri Lanka: with 19,490 living in Ontario; 1,015 in Alberta and 950 in British Columbia; 3,200 in Quebec.

Immigrants from Pakistan total 25,180: with 17,120 living in Ontario; 2,650 in Alberta; 2,720 in Quebec; 1,810 in British Columbia.

From Bangladesh 4,375 immigrants: with 2,455 in Ontario; 1,400 in Quebec; 240 in Alberta and the rest in other provinces.

Only 125 immigrants in Canada are from Nepal with 95 living in Ontario; 15 in British Columbia and 10 in Alberta. The above figures are from the 1991 census. (There is no listing for Bhutan and the Maldives.)

While the people coming to us from these countries are diverse, they must be looked at as people, as individual people, each with his or her own process with his or her own grid or background.

If we are to communicate meaningfully in terms of the message we want to communicate, we need to understand the recipient's socio-cultural, historical, theological and spiritual background. (See **Diagram 1** below)

Diagram 1

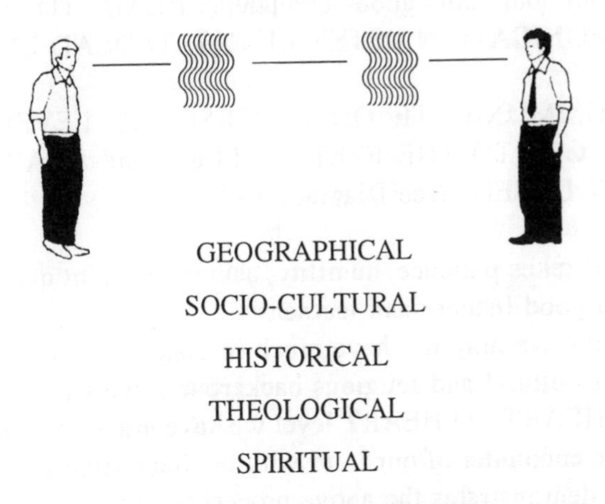

(ADAPTED FROM A DIAGRAM BY FRED FRIESEN)

We can learn a lot about the individual's culture, religion, country, etc. from books. However, the best source is the individual himself or herself. This is how we can personally get to know him/her in terms of their personal belief, cultural background, past history, etc.

In **Diagram 2** Vivian Stacy, a missionary in Pakistan for many years, emphasizes the need to get to know the individual on a personal level.

Diagram 2

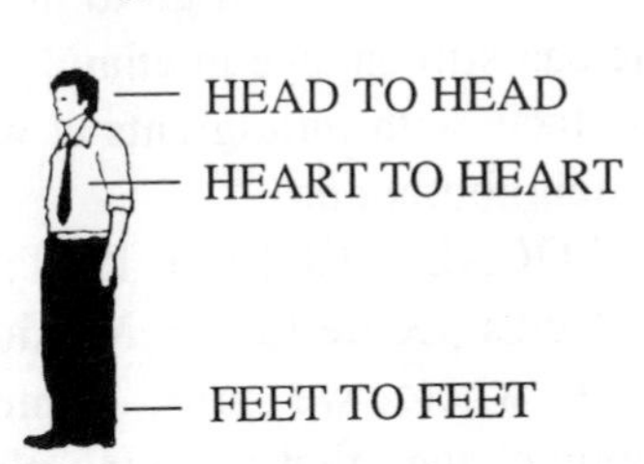

Getting to know the individual HEAD TO HEAD is important but not good enough. HEAD TO HEAD COMMUNICATION OFTEN LEADS TO DEAD ENDS.

TO COMMUNICATE ON A PERSONAL LEVEL WE MUST GET TO THE FEET TO FEET, and HEART TO HEART LEVEL. (see **Diagram 2**)

This takes patience, humility, asking the right questions, being a good listener and learner.

While we may not have much in common with another person's cultural and religious background, we will find that on the HEART TO HEART level we have much in common.

The encounter of our Lord with the Samaritan woman in John 4 demonstrates the above process.

The Need For Preparation

When we moved to Calgary in 1987 we had a two fold objective. One was to work towards starting a church among immigrants. The other, which I felt was more important, was to work with Caucasian evangelical churches. The Lord has brought them to us so that we can help them to catch the vision for ethnic ministry.

Not every Christian can go to the mission field overseas but he/she can still engage in ethnic ministry through his/her natural contacts with immigrants at work, school, university and their neighborhoods.

THE LOCAL CHURCH IS THE KEY in terms of preparing God's people for the **Missions Within Reach.**

This is where we must come to terms with the demographic change that is taking place in our society, and the implications of change... our fears... prejudices... ignorance, etc.

There are three things the church must do in terms of preparing its people:

1. Education

This needs to take place at the local church level. The study of other cultures, religions, countries, can take place in the local church at various levels. The adult Sunday school is a good place to start, offering such a course as an elective. We have taught such a course in a number of churches. Other departments of the church could introduce similar studies with a modified format.

2. Preparation

a. Prepare some in the church to receive those who do come to church. Learn how to make them feel welcome and at home. Do not be eager to invite your Muslim or Hindu friends to church. It is better to develop a friendship with them before starting Bible study with them at home. Introducing them to the church could wait.

b. Prepare leadership in the church to integrate and involve new comers into the life of the church.

c. Prepare everyone in the church to love and accept new comers as a world Christian.

3. Application

Introduce ideas to help your local church to formulate specific objectives for ethnic ministries:

... Some could learn how to teach English-as-a-second-language (ESL)

... Women can exchange cooking lessons.

... Organize a discovery tour: including a visit to a mosque; a tour of the Hindu or Sikh temple; dining out at restaurants serving ethnic food.

... Host an international pot-luck supper.

Possible Models for Church Planting Among South Asians

Immigrants from South Asia are very different from those of other regions (such as Koreans, Filipinos, etc.). Therefore, church planting among them would require a unique strategy that is different from that of other ethnic groups. Church planting models which work well with other ethnic groups may not be applicable to South Asians without due modifications. The two models presented below emerged from years of personal observation and ministry experience among South Asians:

1. Mothering A South Asian Ministry

Mothering a South Asian ministry requires good **planning** and **preparation** and usually is a hard and long **process**.

What does it involve?

... It obviously involves the preliminary process outlined under the section **The Need for Preparation**.

... The viability of such a church planting plan depends largely on the population concentration and the choice of cite or location. The presence of a significant number of people from the same people group in your church neighborhood would be another factor.

... Once the decision has been made, make the daughter church a vital extension of the mother church; don't just provide a place to hold meetings.

... The core group should naturally grow out of the process of friendship evangelism, small Bible study groups, discipline etc.

... Provide support in terms of encouragement, guidance, finance, etc.

... Integrate the new work with the mother church at the Church Board level; programmers for the Sunday School, Youth work and for adults where it may be possible.

Benefits of such a model

... It creates a non-threatening environment and context for new comers.

... It provides the opportunity for the older generation and younger people who do not have the language, to worship in their own language.

... The ministry can be contextualized in terms of preaching, worship, counselling, etc.

... The link with the mother church helps make the transition from the ETHNIC CHURCH TO THE MAIN STREAM CHURCH EASIER. The link also provides for stability. Ethnic churches seem to be plagued with division.

... It can aid the mother church develop skills in cross-cultural ministries.

... It helps the missions emphasis in the mother church to be more dynamic.

2. The International Church Model

The International Church model is an experiment growing out of the need for a church made up of people from different nationalities. We chose this way because:

a. Since we were starting from scratch, it was easier to develop our own philosophy of ministry. We could not go to an existing Caucasian church and expect it to adopt our vision and drastically change their own ministry.

b. We chose the above model to avoid the ghetto mentality by seeking to maintain a good mix of Caucasians and other nationalities.

c. This model best demonstrates the nature of the body of Christ.

How we got started

The Lord had been preparing the way for such a ministry.

... My wife and I who have been in pastoral/missionary work with the Evangelical Missionary Church of Canada for many years felt led of the Lord to move to Calgary to start such a ministry. We shared our vision with our District and were assured of their support. Friendship Ministries was formed to give leadership to this work.

... There were a number of families living in Calgary who had a burden for such a ministry. Together we formed a core group.

... We started with sharing our vision with pastors in the North East Calgary. As mentioned previously, our vision was to work with churches, preparing and equipping them to be involved in cross-cultural ministry. We also worked on reaching South Asians ourselves.

... We started having monthly International Christian Fellowship suppers. This grew and became an outreach to many non-Christians.

... Out of the core group, made up of those families who shared our vision and the growing contacts through the suppers, after three years we started having a Sunday service.

... In January of this year we officially formed the International Church with 26 charter members. It is affiliated with the Evangelical Missionary Church of Canada.

... This church is growing and has seen a number of Hindus come to the Lord and be baptized.

Benefits of such a model

... It creates a non-threatening environment and context for new comers.

... It provides a contextualized ministry in terms of preaching, worship and counselling.

... As the number of people from a given group grows, separate Bible study groups could be formed in their own language.

... **Diagram 3** gives an overview of the philosophy and mission of the church.

Diagram 3

A CHURCH FOR ALL NATIONS TO ALL NATIONS

EFFECTS / EFFECTS / EFFECTS

I. ITS COMMISSION = IT EXISTS TO FULFILL CHRIST'S MISSION - MATTHEW 28:18-20
GO INTO ALL THE WORLD ... MAKE FOLLOWERS ... BAPTIZE ... TEACH ... GO ...

II. ITS COMPOSITION = ONE CHURCH MADE UP OF PEOPLE FROM ALL NATIONS WITH A PERSONALIZED MINISTRY TO EACH LANGUAGE GROUP.

III. ITS COMMITMENT =

1. To worship ... A WORSHIPPING PEOPLE
2. To Fellowship ... A CARING PEOPLE
3. To Discipleship ... EQUIPPING PEOPLE
4. To Stewardship ... A RESPONSIBLE PEOPLE
5. To Evangelism
6. To Missions

A COMMITTED PEOPLE

3. The Eventual Integration

My strong conviction of an eventual integration approach is not without reason. The following is a brief summary of the rationale behind it.

a. It is a hard and long process.

Church planting among South Asian immigrants is not easy, especially among those with the predominant faiths in South Asia, e.g. Islam, Hinduism, Sikhism and Buddhism. The longer they are here, settling into their own community, the more difficult it is to reach them. Church planting among any one of these people or faith groups could take years and would require a lot of patience and hard work.

One-on-one friendship evangelism, small group Bible study, discipline believers and eventually integrating them into a church may be the way to go.

b. Smaller population base and fewer converts.

The relatively smaller number of South Asian immigrants, as compared to the Chinese and Vietnamese, have definitely fewer converts due to the difficulty, as compared to other ethnic groups such as Koreans and Singaporeans who have more exposure prior to immigration and more receptive to the Gospel with fewer cultural and social barriers.

c. The urgent need of fellowship of new converts.

The small number of South Asian new converts (who come from countries with mutual suspicion, deep-rooted hostility, linguistic differences) with heterogeneity (in contrast to the homogeneity of Koreans and Singaporeans) would require a long-time and much effort to cultivate solidarity. In the mean time, the new believers are deprived of fellowship and the discipleship process is delayed.

d. The family unit and newer generation.

Another reason for the approach of integration is the fact that an exclusively South Asian church will eventually lose its local-born English speaking young people and the extended family of multi-generation levels.

Integration of Social Action with Redemptive Love

A strong evangelical presence in terms of meeting the needs of immigrants is lacking. The Mennonite Central Committee is doing a good work in this area.

The needs, of both new immigrants and of those who have been here for longer period, may vary yet their needs must be met. Government and private agencies are not able to meet their needs, making their integration into the main stream culture difficult but ALSO CREATES SOCIAL PROBLEMS.

Areas such as:

... Language proficiency...the need for ESL.

... Employment...learning how to look for work...where to look...how to get Canadian experience...how to get retrained...

... The area of family life is an on-going need. The husband/wife relationship; parent/children relationship; the extended family and it's role.

... Integration into society.

Needs in these areas of need provide opportunities for Christians to minister to them with the love of Christ in practical ways.

The Benefits of a Positive Response

How we respond as evangelical churches to the change that is taking place in Canada's cultural make-up is vital.

1. To respond positively to the change is to be in step with what God is doing in our world today. To ignore what is happening is to expose ourselves to the disease that Peter Wagner identifies as "ethnikitis" and defines as "a static church in a changing neighborhood." Static churches eventually die.

2. To respond positively is to experience a growing vitality and to demonstrate the true nature of the body of Christ.

3. World missions will become a meaningful and dynamic part of the life of the church.

Chapter 6

ETHNIC AND ANGLO CHURCHES IN PARTNERSHIP

Kenneth B. Birch and Eusebio Perez

The prophet Isaiah saw a vision of "the Day of the Lord" when God's perfect rule will be established in Jerusalem and "all nations will stream to it." (Isa. 2:2) God's saving mission in the Old Testament is pictured as being achieved in relationship to a particular people (Israel) and a particular place (Jerusalem). We know from the full revelation of Scripture that the salvation is ultimately accomplished through the work of Christ on the cross. The operative word for God's missionaries today is not "come" but "go" - "Go and preach the gospel...go and make disciples."

Of course, the complete fulfillment of "the Day of the Lord" is still in the future. But the words of this verse capture a fascinating aspect of a Canadian reality in our day. All nations are literally streaming into this country as hundreds of thousands of immigrants leave the familiar, albeit difficult, settings of their native countries to seek the security and prosperity they believe awaits them here. The presentations in this Conference abundantly document the nature and extent of this enormous influx of nation groups. More than 150 of these groups have settled in Toronto alone.

Canada is a far cry from the prophetic picture of Mount Zion where the word of the Lord goes forth and people are taught His ways. The only fulfillment of this prophecy we can see in our day is through the faithfulness and ministry of the Church, the new Israel. But this is precisely the challenge that we wish to sound in this discussion of "Ethnic and Anglo Churches in Partnership".

Definition of Terms

A few important assumptions are foundational to this topic. The first is that "partnership" is, first and foremost, a spiritual reality for those who are related to Jesus Christ. We are members of one Body. We are called to celebrate that unity in Jesus Christ and to live out its practical implications. That means, among other things, partnership in ministry.

Another assumption is that partnership is between equals. We are speaking here again of an essential spiritual reality. Western missionaries have been forced to think through and work through the implications of this over decades of cross-cultural ministry in what we have called the third world. But now Canadian Christians are called upon to deal with pride and ethnocentrism in a new context, the context of working with Christians from other nation groups on Canadian soil.

It is also important to clarify the terms "ethnic" and "anglo" as we are using them in this presentation. These were the terms given to us in the assignment to identify the groups that we represent as working together in partnership in the work of Christ. They have been used among most churches to differentiate between the majority of Canadians whose mother tongue is English and immigrant populations who speak other languages.

Most leaders and writers in the field of minority issues today have recognized the inadequacy of this terminology. Strictly speaking, all Canadians are "ethnic", including Anglophones and Francophones. Therefore, it is quite appropriate that the word "ethnic" has fallen into disfavour. We see this, for example, even in the sub-title of this gathering, "An Intercultural Ministries National Conference". We use the word "ethnic" in our presentation only as a matter of convenience in view of its established traditional meaning.

The challenge we wish to address is that of seeing churches of believers from other cultural groups authentically planted and taking root in Canadian soil. The undeniable reality is that people from Canada's founding nations (French and English) will continue to be dominant numerically for the foreseeable future. Christians from other nation groups will have to make many cultural adjustments in pursuing a new life here. But we need to ask "what adjustments do anglo Christians and churches need to make in order to encourage and facilitate the growth of the Church of Jesus Christ among these new Canadian populations?" We are faced with the necessity of understanding and adjustment on both sides if ethnic churches are to be successfully planted here.

Our goal should be to see a true partnership in the planting and development of ethnic congregations in Canadian soil. We will examine various practical and strategic issues in this partnership between anglo and ethnic churches. Our primary illustrations will be taken from the experiences of Spanish language congregations that are being planted and developed within the structure of the Pentecostal Assemblies of Canada (P.A.O.C.). Generally, the same principles apply where Francophone and Spanish churches establish partnerships.

Preparation for Partnership

Spiritual preparation is the most important element in preparing the ground for a partnership between an Anglophone congregation and an ethnic group in the same area. For the anglophone congregation, it will often mean that a pastor will need to specifically point out how obedience to the Great Commission must begin at home. In the past, when most evangelicals in Canada were born into and grew up in almost totally homogeneous white anglo-saxon communities, obedience to the Great Commission meant "witnessing to your neighbours". Missions meant going great distances to reach people of radically different races and cultures.

In Canada today, of course, the paradigm has changed. Approximately 60% of evangelical Christians now live and attend church in Canada's urban areas where we are confronted with the cultural mosaic everyday. Canada has become a nation of nations. The mission fields have come to our neighbourhoods and we are well aware that this mix, and often clash, of cultures presents real challenges to be worked through for Canadians. That is why spiritual preparation needs to be a priority for Canadian evangelical leaders if we are going to reach these new Canadians. Pastors need to help their people to work through the fears and prejudices that get established, often subtly, in our spirits. It's a new day when obedience to the Great Commission, in terms of cross-cultural evangelism, requires only crossing the street rather than the ocean.

It needs to be understood that a similar preparation needs to be going on within groups of new Canadian "ethnic" believers. It is understandable that ethnic people find great comfort and strength as they associate with their own people in the process of adjusting to a new homeland with all of its differences. The importance of community is even magnified for Christians who share not only cultural but spiritual bonds with fellow country-men and -women.

Spiritual leaders among ethnic groups have the challenge of encouraging these little flocks not to become ghettoized within the Body of Christ. It is important that ethnic believers make the effort to understand and participate in their new adopted homeland and develop new bonds of fellowship with other Christian groups in Canada. As well, there are practical issues of integration, both social and spiritual, which must be dealt with. Some of these will be touched on a little later in this presentation.

Strategic Planning

Once the need for spiritual preparation is addressed, anglo and ethnic leaders must move on to strategic preparation and planning. (It is understood that spiritual and attitudinal development is an ongoing process in the hearts and minds of believers on both sides of the partnership. Strategic preparation should not be unduly delayed in the unrealistic hope that everyone is going to come a place of total spiritual maturity with reference to these issues.)

Looking first at the anglophone congregation, the church that wants to fulfill its responsibility to obey the Great Commission must include planning for ethnic evangelism and church planting in its own "Jerusalem and Judea". If demographic predictions are correct, at least 40% of the population of our cities will be "ethnic" by the end of this century. We can't pretend we are planning to win Canada for Christ if we don't plan to reach our cities. And we can't pretend that we are planning to reach our cities if we aren't planning to reach the large ethnic populations within them.

Some models of church planting will be discussed below. But there are probably two consistent key factors which have triggered successful ethnic outreaches from Canadian anglophone churches. The first is anglo leaders who not only have a vision for cross-cultural evangelism but have also developed and implemented plans. The second is a key ethnic leader, associated with the anglo church, who becomes the primary "builder" for the new congregation. In fact, it will often be a strong personality from an ethnic minority group within a missionary-minded anglo congregation who becomes the stimulus for that church to get moving in ethnic ministry in their immediate area. Fortunate is the church which has such people in their fellowship. And wise is the pastor who recognizes the potential of such people and releases them to reach out to their own people for the sake of the Kingdom of God.

Among the hundreds of thousands of immigrants coming to our shores are those who have been successful Christian leaders - pastors and evangelists - in their home countries. God has already prepared them to lead in reaping the harvest among ethnic populations here in Canada. However, the need for "partnership" is often not strongly felt or understood by these people. And yet it is important, both biblically and practically, that they find a spiritual family and framework within which to work. At the same time, anglophone pastors and leaders need to make a special effort to understand and adjust to thinking and ways of these ethnic brothers and sisters so that ethnocentrism will not kill relationship and potential fruitfulness for the building up of the Body of Christ.

Models of Partnership

1. Sharing of Facilities With Anglo Congregations

From a practical viewpoint, the most important factor in establishing a new ethnic congregation, next to leadership, is the facility in which the group will meet. We know that spiritually and theologically it is the people and not the building that constitutes the essence of the Church. But on a practical level, a "place" for the Body of Christ to come together is important. This is probably of greater concern to ethnic minorities trying to establish a local congregation than it is to anglophones in this day of "Consumer Christianity" where denominations and buildings are decreasing in importance.

Many anglophone churches have facilities that are used only a few hours each week. If the pastor has a vision to reach a nearby ethnic population, he or she might look for an ethnic leader to start a new congregation. Or an ethnic pastor who has identified a location to plant a new congregation might approach the leadership of an anglophone church with a proposal for the use of their facilities.

The arrangement might involve free use or a rental fee or an evolving situation where financial requirements are tied to the growth of the ethnic congregation. Whatever the case, experience has taught us the importance of having very clear communication and agreements "up front" before entering in to this kind of arrangement.

The reality is that most non-anglophone cultures have very different patterns of worship, socializing and organization. For example, the worship of Spanish Pentecostal churches is much noisier and more demonstrative than mainstream Canadian pentecostalism. The services are much longer and the people love to stay around and visit for long periods of time after the services. Often, the control of children during these times is not a major concern. And then there is often food associated with social times. If the ethnic congregation meets in the afternoon, the odors of ethnic foods can easily linger until the time that the anglophone congregation returns for an evening service.

Ideally, there has been a good deal of spiritual and attitudinal preparation among the anglophone congregation before the ethnic work begins. But even if the host congregation has been somewhat prepared to welcome a fledgling ethnic congregation into its facilities, it is still essential that there be clear understandings going in to such an arrangement. In fact, growing evangelical churches with full calendars of activities would do well to take a long hard look at whether or not such an arrangement with an ethnic congregation is feasible. Agreements need to be clearly talked through and written out. Both groups need to establish liaison people at high levels to communicate on behalf of both parties. There are some sad stories of relationships between anglo and ethnic congregations that have deteriorated because both sides failed to adequately plan and count the cost before entering in to shared arrangements.

Another key element in a relationship between Anglo and ethnic congregations is the relationship between pastors. It should not be concluded from what was said above that the ideal is strike a purely "business" relationship. Occasionally we find the strong ethnic leader who is secure and astute enough that he or she can function on that basis. But ethnic churches seldom flourish where there isn't some kind of spiritual, moral and perhaps even financial support that comes from the host church. Some of the healthiest ethnic churches hosted in anglo churches have developed when the anglo pastor has given some regular priority time to encourage and nurture his or her ethnic colleague.

2. The Role of District and National Offices

It should be assumed, hopefully, that denominational headquarters offices have a burden and vision for reaching ethnic as well as anglophone communities within their sphere of responsibility. Most denominations today have done demographic studies to determine where certain ethnic groups are locating in relation to their existing local churches or in relation to sites targeted for church planting.

We recognize that there are different types of polity within evangelical groups which will largely determine where the initiative comes from for ethnic church planting. The models we are discussing here are based on the structure of the Pentecostal Assemblies of Canada which we call a "Cooperative Fellowship". In this system, church planting is a normally a cooperative effort between existing local churches, district offices and, occasionally, the national office, working in some type of joint venture.

The models referred to above have mostly been based on local church initiative, or the initiative of an entrepreneurial ethnic leader. In some of these cases, local pastors have been encouraged by district or national leaders to move in the direction of ethnic church planting even though these administrative offices and their officials have not become directly involved in these projects.

There are many examples, on the other hand, where district and national offices have had a major, direct role in the establishing of new ethnic churches. These offices should be able to keep the "big picture" in view concerning patterns of immigration and where these new Canadians are settling within their jurisdictions.

There are times when the leadership of a local anglophone church has a burden and vision to reach a nearby ethnic population but does not have the resources to initiate this type of ministry. In such cases, the district and/or national offices may be approached to set up a joint venture.

Often this will mean, first of all, finding the right church planting pastor for the new ethnic congregation. Then the appropriate plans and structure need to be put in place. The key element is a "Steering Committee" comprised of representatives of the various sponsoring groups - local, district and national - plus the church planting pastor and, hopefully, one or more founding lay leaders from the new ethnic congregation.

In cases where there is a lack of vision in an existing local anglophone church to reach out to ethnic populations within their area, the district and national offices may consult together and pool resources to make a church plant possible. The nearest local church will always be consulted but their approval and involvement is not an absolute requirement. Often such support will come after the project has proven to be viable.

As always, the key to a successful plant is the right leader. Here again, the appropriate administrative officer will often be in a position to find such a person. In some cases a person with a suitable background may already be in Canada. Or it may be necessary to recruit someone from the homeland where the majority of people in this cultural group have come from.

Once the appropriate structure is in place and the leader found, the next concern is a location for the church to begin. In the absence of support or an invitation from an existing anglophone church, a neutral facility, such as a school or a community center, is rented for services.

Of course, finances are always a major issue in this type of project. We have found that, as a rule, the same approach and policies used on overseas mission fields are applicable when planting ethnic churches in Canada. Normally, sponsoring bodies should commit to support the new ethnic congregation for a period of not more than five years on a reducing scale over the period of the commitment. For example, if there are three sponsoring bodies (a local church, a district office and a national office), each of those sponsors might begin with a commitment of $1,000 per month for the first year, reducing this amount by $200 per month in each of the succeeding years. In other words, the total support goes from $3,000 per month in the first year down to $600 per month in the fifth year. It is assumed, of course, that teaching on tithing is part of the discipline process from the very formation of this new congregation. In some cases, we have been able to discontinue subsidies for new ethnic churches after the third year.

3. Ethnic (Cultural) Fellowships

What happens when a denomination arrives at the point of having several congregations of the same ethnic or cultural groups across the country? Is it necessary or beneficial to form some kind of organization to coordinate these churches? In our experience, the answer is "yes".

Denominational polity will usually dictate the framework within which these new works are integrated. In the case of the P.A.O.C., all church bodies and credential holders are under the jurisdiction of the district offices. But the denomination has decided that, in addition to the governmental structure provided by the district, it is advantageous for these developing ethnic congregations, and their pastors, to have a more informal "fellowship" structure to serve the spiritual and practical needs of these groups.

P.A.O.C. by-laws provide for the formation of a "Language Fellowship" whenever a particular language or cultural group has a sufficient number of congregations, usually meaning 8 or more. (The title is currently being changed from "language" to "cultural" to reflect the reality that culture rather than language is a more accurate way to distinguish these groups.) The major functions of this "fellowship" structure are:

a. to provide fellowship, teaching and inspiration to leaders and members of these congregations;
b. to provide consultation and resources to assist these congregations in their outreach and development;
c. through "national coordinators", to provide direction in identifying the locations where new works may be needed among these cultural populations;
d. national coordinators also serve as liaisons to district executives in credentialling and disciplining pastors within the particular cultural group.

The cultural groups immigrating to Canada inevitably face the issue of changing values and behaviour patterns in the second, third and succeeding generations. Of course, the church is not exempt from having to deal with this reality. While this is not the place to deal with all of the implications of this complicated issue, suffice it to say that flexibility is essential in developing policies for ethnic churches.

Almost always, the day will come when the children and youth of cultural congregations will become part of anglophone (now multi-cultural!) congregations. And there will almost always be a degree of generational tension and conflict when this happens.

The resolution of the difficulties must be left in the hands of the leaders of these minority groups. Our point here is that, when working out partnerships between anglo and ethnic congregations, serious attention should be paid to structure the relationship in such a way as to facilitate this generational shift.

Conclusion

Whatever may be the current rate of growth or decline among churches in Canada today, the future trend will almost certainly be one of decline, especially in urban areas, unless church leaders plan for aggressive evangelism and church planting among our growing ethnic populations. There are numbers of ethnic churches that are reaching their own cultural groups independently (ie. without a working relationship with anglophone congregations or denominations.) Some ethnic leaders feel this is the preferable route to establish ministries that will relate authentically to their own people.

That argument fails for at least three reasons. First, it denies, in appearance at least, the spiritual reality of the inter-relatedness of the Body of Christ. Christians are called to live out that relationship in our corporate life and ministry. Secondly, it fails to prepare the ethnic church to deal with the realities of integration into the Canadian environment. This failure becomes especially evident in the difficulties of adjustment faced by the children of Christians from ethnic minorities. Thirdly, it fails to allow for the sharing of resources - spiritual, human, financial, etc. - which can often mean the difference between a strong or weak beginning for ethnic churches and perhaps even ultimate success or failure.

A possible concern among ethnic leaders (and these people are often too gracious to verbalize this) is that anglo leadership might want to control the development of the ethnic work. Will there be a true partnership of equals? The answer to this question relates to the attitude of anglo church leaders. This paper presentation has been prepared with the assumption that these leaders have a genuinely open and accepting attitude towards ethnic minorities and a willingness to allow ethnic churches to develop in ways that are both biblical and authentic to their own culture.

There is potential for a great spiritual harvest among the hosts of new Canadians that are arriving daily. It is our conviction that the best way for this harvest to be reaped is for an effective partnership of ethnic and anglo church leaders. (Of course, the same type of partnership is needed in French Canada between ethnic and francophone leaders). As in any successful venture for God, the first need is for **vision.** If that vision is truly from the Holy Spirit, it will be accompanied by a **passion** to reach them with the gospel. This vision and passion must ultimately result in a plan of action which will provide preachers and church planters to fulfill God's plan.

Chapter 7

A CASE STUDY OF THE FIRST FILIPINO BAPTIST CHURCH, TORONTO

Eliezer Catanus

Introduction

It is a distinct honor to be invited to participate in this workshop. I will be presenting about the church that I have been privileged to be its pastor for almost eleven years. We will discuss its history, its sociological, theological/biblical bases, the distinct characteristics of its ministries, and its vision for the future.

This case study, however, does not presume to be the best there is of a local church, for I know fully well the weaknesses of this church. Ours is only one of the many models that might be adopted for the carrying out of the Great Commission.

Its History

Nestled in downtown Toronto, mingling with the bustling stores, fast food eateries and residential homes, the First Filipino Baptist Church stands as a monument of faith to a crowd of almost three hundred worshippers. Every Sunday believers comprising mostly of Filipinos who either make use of Toronto's transit system or drive from the nearby suburbs, wind their way to this house of worship. For fourteen years this edifice situated in 382 Lippincott Street has been the venue for worship service, prayer service, fellowship meeting, wedding, Bible study and child dedication.

Eighteen years ago on September 9, 1975, the First Filipino Baptist Church was born in seed form. Four Filipino immigrants, all college graduates in the Philippines, motivated by God's love and desire to grow in Christ, came together to encourage one another through prayer and Bible study. Through their Friday meetings, the group increased in number.

They reached out to friends and co-workers who either dropped by out of curiosity or sought something different from the usual Friday activities. Pretty soon the apartment which housed their regular fellowships could no longer hold their growing number. They moved to a larger place, this time they met at the faculty lounge of the West Park Secondary School at Bloor and Dundas.

It was on Easter Sunday of April 17, 1977 at the High Park Baptist Church when they decided to organize themselves as a church. With the guidance and encouragement of Rev. Melvin Donald, Dr. Timothy Starr and Dr. George Bell, and with the financial support of the Fellowship of Evangelical Baptist Churches in Canada Home Missions, the group asked Godfrey Catanus, then a Filipino student of the Central Baptist Seminary, to pastor the newly-formed church. On May 15, 1977, the first Sunday worship service was held at the Bonar Park Presbyterian Church where thirty-six baptized believers, mostly young professionals, became the church's chartered members.

On June 25, 1977, the first business meeting was held with the election of the first church officers. The church recognition service was held on October 14, 1977 with the attendance of representatives from fellowshipping Baptist churches. The First Filipino Baptist Church was officially accepted as member of the Fellowship of Evangelical Baptist Churches in Canada at its annual convention in October 24, 1977. On July 28, 1978, the church rented the building at 382 Lippincott Street, Toronto, once a conference center of the Salvation Army, which the Fellowship purchased. The church dedication service in this building followed on December 12, 1978. Pastor Godfrey Catanus was ordained as the First Filipino Baptist minister in Canada on May 15, 1979. With Pastor Godfrey's resignation on August 21, 1981, Rev. Eliezer Catanus, his older brother, was called by the church to succeed him. Pastor Eliezer Catanus and his family came from the Philippines to Toronto on December 29, 1981. Through God's grace, the church became financially viable that she could fully support the pastor and pay-off the mortgage. In 1985, the Fellowship transferred the property under the ownership of the First Filipino Baptist Church.

It was a real joy to see the ministry growing that in 1990 our membership broke the 250 barrier. Sensing the real need of more space for worship and ministries, the church launched a major building renovation project. There were "giants in the land": the deepening economic recession, many of our people were laid off from their jobs, the inner city parking and zoning bylaws, and the biggest giant of all - the pessimism of some of our church people. But against all these odds, the mighty faith of the majority of our people overcame the "giants". Our $750,000 renovation project was finished after six moths of construction, all financed by our members. We inaugurated our new building on October 4, 1992. All glory be to God!

Sociological Basis

The First Filipino Baptist Church's ministry started from the sociological level. It was primarily directed towards the Filipino community. The four young Filipino Christian professionals felt that the Filipino group would address to their needs and the needs of those who prefer to worship in a Filipino context. They were in a unique position to reach out to the unsaved Filipinos for generally Filipino could best relate to fellow Filipinos.

The following are the sociological/cultural reasons for the Filipino or ethnic ministry in Toronto:

a. Filipinos worship in a context that is different from that which is normally encountered in established churches in Toronto.

   Some of these differences are the following: Filipinos are spontaneously bilingual and speak English or the native Filipino language with equal facility. Thus we may choose to pray, sing, preach or share in either language depending on the leading of the Holy Spirit. In addition, there are many dialects that also may be used before, during, and after worship. Secondly, Filipinos personally are by nature shy. When forced to joint with a North American worship service in English, they often feel intimidated into remaining quiet. Thirdly, Filipinos worship in a spontaneous manner, and do not mind going over the time allotted for a worship service, a practice often incompatible and often unacceptable in a North American context. Fourthly, music is an important part of the Filipino worship service, and music may include Filipino hymns and choruses.

b. In a Filipino context, each person's potential to serve the Lord can be more fully expressed and realized. We expect this to be so for no one understands a Filipino better than another Filipino. Thus the concerted effort of evangelical Filipinos would be the most effective or relevant way to bring the Gospel of salvation to the unsaved among us.

c. Filipino ministry in the Philippines traditionally encompasses the whole worship day, not to mention the mid-week ministries. This zeal for the Lord arises from a deep-seated concern of Filipinos for each other. In the Canadian milieu, the Filipino is confronted with the whirlwind lifestyle that is not normally encountered in the more genteel Filipino society. Because the immigrant Filipino in Canada often becomes too busy to be fully committed to the Lord's work, we feel that a Filipino church can best preserve his zeal and dedication to the Lord.

d. The Lord's command to us is to go and make disciples of all nations, teaching them to obey all that He has commanded (Matthew 28:19-20).

   Discipleship involves a close interaction and deep personal concern among the fellowship of believers. We believe therefore that discipleship can be more effective in a Filipino local church where Filipinos would disciple other Filipinos. We feel that this type of ethnic ministry will be used of God as an example to the other ethnic communities of greater Toronto so that God's Word will be spread even faster.

Theological/Biblical Basis

Dr. J.H. Bavinck said, "...The Bible repeatedly refers to the entire world, in all its fullness, including all who dwell therein, as a creation of God... Genesis 1:1 is obviously the necessary basis of the Great Commission of Matthew 28:19-20." [1]

Psalm 47:1 and 99:1 summon not only the nation of Israel but all nations to honor God. The nations according to the psalmist are subject to God's righteousness and He demands their obedience. All nations are forbidden to worship and serve other gods. The God of the Scriptures is the only true and living God (Jeremiah 10:1-6).[2]

Ezekiel the prophet foresaw the reconciliation of the nations and the restoration of relationship with God through His overture of grace which all peoples of the world would take part (Genesis 3:1-15; Ezekiel 36:22-23). Ezekiel in his prophetic message implies that God will call the nations to be His glorified people and through Christ, they will share in His salvation.

The Apostle Peter called the church "a holy nation". This "holy nation" is composed of people form different nations, races, and cultures. The unifying factor of the "holy nation" is the Lord Jesus Christ. [3]

The Apostle John described the eschatological gathering of this "holy nation" when he said: "...I looked and there before me was a great multitude that no one could count, form every nation, tribe, people and language, standing before the throne and in front of the Lamb... they cried out in a loud voice: `Salvation belongs to God, who sits on the throne, and to the Lamb'... They fell down on their faces before the throne and worshipped God, saying: `Amen'! Praise and glory and wisdom and thanks and honor and power and strength be to our God forever and ever Amen!" (Rev.7:9-12, NIV).

It is obvious that The First Filipino Baptist Church began with the "homogenous unit principle". Filipinos reaching out to fellow Filipinos just developed naturally for the first ten years of the church life. But in the next eight years, as the church matures spiritually, the members have started reaching out to non-Filipinos. This too develops naturally. We have just started on our development towards a multi-cultural church. Less than one percent of our membership are non-Filipinos and we absolutely have a long way to go. Nevertheless, three non-Filipinos are serving on the Board of Directors, the chairman is Spanish and two members have Anglo-saxon background. And let me add: these three are doing their job very well!

Distinctive Characteristics of Its Ministries

1. In Evangelizing

Although the congregation believes that we should not only be evangelical but also evangelistic, only about fifteen percent of our members are consistently evangelizing. One-on-one witnessing, friendship, and lifestyle evangelism are the most common methods of evangelizing. Friendship evangelism, so far, has been the most effective type of evangelism in the Filipino community. This is because of the fact that generally, Filipinos are friendly by nature. Filipino immigrants and contract workers, many of whom come to Canada alone, leaving their families back home and therefore lonely and are in need of help. These people are quite responsive to friendship and lifestyle evangelism. We have at present 21 Home Bible study groups around Metro

Toronto. These are avenues for caring, evangelism and discipleship. Most of our visitors come every Sunday morning because of a friend from the Bible study groups.

Aware of this reality, our Sunday morning preaching would almost often end with an evangelistic appeal. The seed of the Word has already been sown in the hearts of many of our visitors. Many of their prejudices and stereotype thinking about evangelical Christianity have been broken down. They become in most cases ripe for the picking.

Filipinos generally are musical. We take advantage of this reality by conducting periodic evangelistic concerts. We encourage our people, the children, young people, and adults to serve with their gifts in music. Through music ministries and friendship, they evangelize and in turn they are edified.

2. In Church Planting

We have planted for the past eleven years three daughter churches, another two are in the process of being organized. Four of these are in Metro Toronto and one is in Hamilton. We have been directly instrumental also in planting five churches in the Philippines, specifically in cities where there are practically no strong evangelical witness. We support national church planters and most of them are really doing the job at a much lesser expense than North American missionary church planters.

Our church planting work in Metro Toronto and Hamilton are in partnership with the Fellowship Home Missions and World Team.

3. In Pastoring/Shepherding

The congregation grew numerically and in 1990, we broke the "two hundred fifty barrier" mark. And as the flock increased in quantity, shepherding demands also increased. We called an Assistant Pastor on a part-time basis for one year. He was an engineer having a good job. But he was so involved in the church work as Sunday School Teacher, Deacon, and choir Director. After a year, he decided to go into full time ministry as Assistant Pastor/Administrator of our church. At the same time, he is taking courses in Seminary toward a theological degree. This relieves the Senior Pastor of many responsibilities and enables him to spend more time in prayer and the ministry of the Word.

Shepherding primarily involves feeding the flock. Therefore, preaching is central in our Sunday celebration. Most Filipinos don't mind a forty five-minute sermon. Expository preaching has been the type of preaching in our church for years. We have gone through the Old Testament and already most of the New Testament. Believing in the inerrancy and sufficiency of the Scriptures, we preach on controversial issues such as abortion, homosexuality, pornography, etc., and examine all views in the light of God's Word. Sunday pulpit preaching has always been characterized by a Filipino flavor, e.g. the use of Filipino illustration, story, proverb, and even the Filipino sense of humor. One thing I am grateful and happy for being a preacher in the Filipino congregation is that I can preach beyond the designated time limitation and still be forgiven.

4. In Counselling

Counselling in our church is more contextualized. By this I mean, you have to really know and understand the Filipino culture and background of the counselee before you can help him/her to come to grips with the Scriptures. How can you help a wife and mother who came to Canada as a nanny, being the only-breadwinner in the family? Counselling a devoted wife who works in Toronto as a nanny, and her husband is fooling around with another woman in the Philippines, is quite tough. About twenty percent of our members are domestic helpers. Problems with immigration, employment, housing and emotional, financial, and spiritual needs arise, demanding careful attention. The pastor by necessity has to learn to meet these needs through contextualized Christian counselling.

Knowledge of both the culture and the Scriptures has proven to be greatly advantageous in this helping relationship. There have been instances where referrals to professional Christian counselors have been necessary.

Its Vision For Future Ministry

There were 194,000 Filipinos in Canada in 1991. It is estimated that this number will increase to 318,000 Filipinos in Canada in 1996 and 477,000 in 2001. There were 492,000 South Asians (Subcontinent of India, Pakistan, Sri Lanka, Bangladesh and Nepal) in 1991 and the projection is that they will reach 1.29 million in 2001. Southeast Asians (people from Indochina, Vietnam, Cambodia, and Laos) were 141,00 in 1991 and will increase to 302,000 in 2002. The blacks (Canadian born, African, Caribbean) were 527,000 two years ago and that will become 1,500,000 of them in 2001. How about the Hispanics? In 1991, Latin Americans were 131,000 in Canada and by 2001 they will increase to 347,000.[4] Most of these people are in the major cities of Canada.

The question that we should ask ourselves in view of this surge of ethnic population growth is: "How can we evangelize our dying cities for the living Christ?" Our vision, as a church at the close of this century and beyond is to plant a church in each of the major cities of Canada. How can we do it? By God's grace, we begin with motivation, leading to mobilization and finally implementation.

1. Motivation

The church leadership should first be motivated. Everything rises or falls on leadership. The pastor, being the key leader in the church, should catch the vision and share it with the leaders. His preaching, his teaching and his lifestyle should reflect his vision. He must be obsessed by his vision that it will become contagious.

2. Mobilization

The second step is to mobilize people to pray. Prayer is supreme in accomplishing God's purpose in world-wide evangelization (Matthew 9:38). Then the church should equip and train motivated leaders to go into ethnic church planting. Anglo members should be trained for cross-cultural evangelism and church planting.

3. Implementation

With prayer permeating the process of motivation, mobilization, actual church planting must occur across Canada. Every venture for the cause of the kingdom of God has a big price tag on it. The church should be willing to pray more, to give more and to send more of its own choice people.

The golden opportunity for evangelism, ethnic or cross-cultural, is now. The world is here in Canada. And we can't afford to miss this opportunity of the century. We have the vision of ethnic or multi-cultural evangelical, evangelistic, and missionary churches in Canada. This is Christ's last command and it is our primary concern.

End Notes

1. The Nations for Christ: Challenge to Canadian Mosaic, A paper read to the student body of North West Bible College, Edmonton, Alberta, during chapel service, September 28, 1990, Rev. Sadiri Joy B. Tira.
2. Ibid.
3. Ibid.
4. Toronto, Star, May 30, 1992.

Chapter 8

The Multicultural Pastorate

Ralph R. Glagau

The Bible sets the tone for every worthwhile endeavour. Acts 6:3 provides a valid reference for our experience and for all cultural interchange. Although the presentation may vary, church problems are basically people problems. The antidote for such is to be of godly character and to be full of the Holy Ghost. These are the Biblical characteristics that are sought after and, while this text does not always receive this application, it is this writer's conviction that only God's ennoblements have afforded us any testimony or example in the field of multiculturalism.

It is important for us to share some of the history of the Humberlea Church of God in order to give our readers a proper perspective. The multicultural milieu and dynamic were intertwined from the outset. The church began in late 1965 when a retired couple with a German background and a rich pastoral experience in the metropolitan Detroit area felt the burden to come to Toronto. They were introduced to a large extended family group from Trinidad who had been introduced to the Church of God before coming to Toronto. The American couple and the West Indian family began renting a church and a house from a German-speaking church group whose membership was in decline. The fourth cultural dynamic was added when an independent Christian group, led by a missionary's son born in Manchuria, came on the scene. It seems that only God could have arranged the foregoing relationship and fellowship and hence, a multicultural church was birthed.

The Humberlea Church has since been a `mother' church to several other churches, mostly of West Indian background, in the Toronto area. The multicultural flavour has continued; in 1985 a visitor observed that in a 27 - voice choir there were 9 blacks, 9 Indians, and 9 Caucasians. Presently, one may find a German-Canadian gentleman, a Mexican-Canadian family, and a Chinese-Canadian couple all sharing a pew on any given Sunday.

The other historical dimension is myself and my family who moved to the pastorate in 1976. I was born and raised on the Canadian Prairies. My father was German and he quickly learned multicultural survival in Saskatchewan when being persecuted during Hitler's horrific reign. The example was, therefore, set for me in my home and in our local church; the poor, the native, and the disenfranchised were always welcome in Dad's home or in his pew at church. God's wisdom in my training was at work. While growing up I felt that mission service would be my goal; however, I never got that far. Although we have had the privilege of visiting several mission fields, a multicultural pastorate seems to be God's place for our family.

We now wish to direct our attention to what we will call the strength of the multicultural church: it encourages acceptance and creativity. People who feel unwelcome in more homogeneous churches often feel at home at Humberlea. Our Church Council has always shown great forbearance and understanding in dealing with the cultural nuances of a Spanish church group that has shared our facilities for about 15 years. In our programming we find ready resources for and enthusiastic responses to interesting events such us a Flag Parade, the Lord's Prayer in 15 languages, and love themes that use placards for each language and/or country of origin.

Without exception, visiting speakers of our own denomination and of various para-church groups respond very positively to the cultural mix and for many it may be their first speaking engagement where they meet face-to-face with such cultural variety.

Let me share the testimony of one of our members who has grown up in the Humberlea church:

> The true worshipping church by `nature' will, by the love of God and the empowering of the Spirit, embrace peoples of all nations within its fellowship and ministry.
>
> Society attempts multiculturalism, plurality, etc. and tries to 'stamp out racism and prejudice'. The church is the place where diversity is celebrated in unity (of the faith - one baptism, one God); where we may come from different lands but are all looking for one land and one city whose maker and builder is God; where the love of God and the example of Christ and the apostles leave no room for racism or prejudice but, rather, demonstrate acceptance and true community of brothers and sisters in Christ.

It would be easier to avoid the next area of discussion, but let us also be aware of the weaknesses that exist, or may exist, in a multicultural church. One which initially comes with most immigrant populations is a financial and educational shortfall. These are people who, for the most part, need to find their own way in a new culture and the immigration process does place some strain on these two areas of life.

The next weakness, sometimes combined to be a strength, are the limitations of some programs. The illustration of this may be an Americanized promotion of teen programs regarding dating. The program may be well-packaged and attractive to a typical homogeneous Canadian church, but it will not create interest and, in fact, will be opposed by families that have arranged children's marriages for years. Many other subtle cultural patterns influence a great deal of the life of the multicultural congregation.

The other area of weakness we wish to mention is that everyone is not in the same place culturally. The difference spreads from those who would accept a mixed marriage between races to those who would not allow their children to attend a multicultural church for fear of a marriage possibility. Another way of expressing this is that you are open to criticism from all sides: from the blacks because you are not all black, from the whites for similar reasons, and from the Latinos because you fail to maintain certain traditions which they hold dear in their home country. This diversity of thought will even appear within family groups, hindering what would appear to be potential for evangelism and growth.

It is certainly necessary for the pastor and the congregation to address these questions for the sake of self-preservation and insulation against the criticisms that will be encountered.

The next area of discussion will center on a more positive topic: capitalizing on the multicultural base for evangelism. When our people go to a park to distribute gospel tracts or conduct door-to-door evangelism, there are some obvious advantages. If the recipient is of any minority group, he will recognize the apparent openness of the group and possibly be more receptive. Also, the church person is usually better equipped, due to his multicultual exposure, to assess the person's background and bias and, hence, communicate better.

For example, when you correctly identify a man with apparent Indian features as a Tamil and are able to offer him a tract in his own language, you have already arrived halfway at a communication level.

Another advantage is that you can use certain ethnic customs for evangelism within the particular family and cultural grouping. Scheduled functions such as baby dedications often attract visitors who are not Christians. In addition to the church service, there is often a family dinner at which time the church people who are present have occasion to witness. Similar opportunities occur at house dedications, home thanksgiving services, weddings, etc. where people who have family and friend connections come under Christian influence and message.

Another opportune focus is the youth of minority families who are looking for Canadian assimilation but feel threatened by a completely homogeneous congregation. In the Humberlea experience, we have often seen this work effectively. We presently have three Spanish-speaking families who attend the English church, although we have a Spanish church of the same denomination in the same location, with the purpose of experiencing an English atmosphere, which is especially advantageous for their children and a cultural milieu that is accepting,and yet not binding, in regards to their country of origin.

The final area to which we wish to make reference is missions or cross-cultural ministry. There is an initial roadblock to overcome in the romanticization of foreign missions. It is important to realize that paternalism is not the most effective approach and may even be counter-productive. Once this is avoided, at least in Humberlea's experience, any cross-cultural ministry is immediately well-accepted and challenging. This has been the case in the home missions scene where our Council members, along with the congregation, have been very open and accepting of experiments in supporting other cultural efforts. This support may vary from an encouraging response to a person who has delivered a mediocre song or a sermon in halted English to the more costly area of supporting a Spanish-speaking church to the tune of several thousands of dollars and not feeling vengeful when failure and misunderstandings cause division.

On this mission theme, the church has also shown great openness to ministry in other lands. Hence, we constantly have fund raising projects and offerings for any number of countries and ministries. A partial list of a year's projects includes: Bibles for China; evangelism in India; support of ministers in Latvia; Haiti, Honduras, and an orphanage in Guatemala; sending aid to the former Soviet Union, Guyana, and Zambia; assisting a preaching and teaching mission to Armenia. This list could continue and yet the cross-cultural ministry always creates goodwill and brings the congregation together as they achieve these goals. In many cases, people are helping to evangelize their own country of origin which adds impetus and significance to the effort. This mission interest has resulted in an increasing mission budget over the years. It has also produced two very fruitful mission trips where 5 and 10 persons respectively participated. The vision that this has given the congregation is still producing results for which we give God praise.

The conclusion of this biography of the multi-cultural pastorate is not going to leave us with pat answers to the standard questions. What of the future in terms of the multi-cultural pastorate? What guidelines and direction can you receive from this study? Only God knows what direction you as a reader needs to move in as far as your personal life and your congregation are concerned. Let me leave you with these final observations as you look to the future. First, let me assure you that a living, dynamic faith and the help of the Holy Spirit as referred to at the start are essential. The people of such a community will be expected to give their all and trust God implicitly, not only for spiritual, but also for social and personal needs as well. Second, I observe the rising of a new generation which may or may not become a domination factor in Canada's social scheme. This generation will find its faith meaningful only in a multi-cultural church or, at least, one that is comfortable in addressing and assimilating such characteristics. Third, I would strongly recommend against faking an interest in such a work or ministry. The cost of involvement would be too great if we only assume an interest without the genuine concern and love for the difficulties and discrepancies that come with the multi-cultural mix. Finally, this main question will probably remain, "Is it relevant for you in the 1990s?" Many factors will vary in this regard - geography, denomination, and personal ambitions - but the determination to keep the Gospel relevant at the close of this century is the challenge awaiting the church.

Chapter 9

PRESENT EFFORTS AND FUTURE STRATEGIES OF THE EVANGELIZATION OF CANADA'S NATIVE POPULATION

Ross W. Maracle

Among Canada's First Nations peoples there is a yearning for chance and upward mobility that is engulfing their societies. There is a cry for nation and leadership in the social, economic, religious and political sectors.

Statistical data, concerning the spiritual condition, health, housing, poverty, suicide, the imprisonment of natives, and resurgence of Native religions,are not hidden. We must take the initiative in intercession, evangelism, social action and legislation to pave the way for a new direction for Native Canadians who are known to have a legacy of sorrow.

The Canadian church has often placed its missions priority on foreign countries. It needs to become near-sighted and see the tens of thousands of natives that are filling our cities. Many are homeless and churchless. They fill detox and rehab centres, jails and halfway houses, but not our churches. Home missions must be re-emphasized with a rethinking of mission strategies.

The church is to be the bastion of morality and the conscience of the nation. It is the church's duty to raise questions of morality to our nation. We have eloquently addressed ourselves to the abortion issue, but what about the more than 400 native youths who commit suicide each year.

After five hundred years of missionary activities, less than four percent of the Native population are considered born again. There is a stirring that something credible, creative and continuing must be done as concerning this great mission field in our midst. We can gain a new ministry perspective by re-evaluating and re-examining our past ministry endeavors to Native people.

Re-Examining Past Ministry Initiatives to Native People

One problem in the evangelization of the native Canadian was that the missionary often with a broad stroke of the brush insensitively classified our culture as pagan. Not everything in traditional native society fits in with Christianity, but native culture is no more inherently pagan than non-native culture with its Easter bunny, Tooth Fairy, Santa Clause and Halloween.

Jesus Christ was often presented in the trapping of the European/Western Culture. However, Jesus Christ must be presented with wisdom in the context of the Native culture. Christ does not necessarily remove a person from their culture - He transforms them within their culture.

We, as Native Christians, don't need non-Native missionaries determining for us with imposition of guilt, as to what is good or bad in our culture. Non-Native people need to trust the Lord who can and will enable us to wisely determine what is good and bad in our culture. However, let me hasten to say that I do not believe in syncretism (i.e. mixing of religions), there is only one element which must never be diluted, i.e. Jesus Christ our Lord.

It should be absolutely mandatory for anyone of non-Native background, considering an ongoing involvement in Native ministry, to be cross-culturally trained. To learn the values and strengths, as well as the Native religion of that particular culture. Look for a Native training program or Bible school that offers seminars or courses on Native spirituality from a Christian viewpoint. What better place is there to be trained than among Natives to reach Natives.

Yes, our vision is being readjusted and refocused. We are not looking out the rear view mirror and seeing the past, we are looking at the present and seeing the need. In the following, I offer a limited overview of some of the critical areas that must increasingly be addressed for greater effectiveness in the area of Native ministry.

The Call to Prayer

Prayer is a non-threatening, unifying and networking vehicle that would channel and focus more effectively the deep spiritual groaning and aspiration of my people. Prayer can be a common denominator and a mechanism for recovery, renewal and reconciliation.

Prayer can have several different foci: leaders, organizations, evangelism, etc. But for any endeavor to minster to Natives must initially be covered by prayer. Often "pre-emptive prayer strike" will have to be launched first because you are going into areas that are often under the control of the enemy and possibly have never been contested with a concerted and continuing Christian effort. It is amazing what tears of the sower will do to soften hardened ground.

Ministry to the Native Family Unit

In any ministry to the Native Canadian, one of the greatest challenges is to identify with the Native family unit. Creatively we must now try and deal with the devastating policy of cultural assimilation that was enacted by the government with good intentions, and perpetuated upon us through the residential schools system that was operated by two religious systems in Canada.

Native children were taken out of their communities and away from their families for 11 and a half months out of the year. In their school nothing native was allowed as in food, language or clothing. Their hair was curled, shoes replaced moccasins and their native names were changed.

It was almost as though their existence was a mistake. This attempted makeover was through forced baptisms, recitals of prayers and anglo-education. What emerged from this misguided attempt to redefine a people was the disfunction of a people group.

It was in these residential schools that non-native statisticians estimate approximately 75-80% of these defenseless children were sexually abused. They returned home with inner turmoil, and identity crisis and a moral system in tatters. Social therapists often say that an abused child many times perpetuates what has happened to him upon others.

Nellie Beardy, executive directors of the Sioux Lookout First Nations Health Authority, says that many young people are feeling fallout from their grandparents and parents harrowing experiences in residential schools.

"Because that generation was taken away from the community," she explained, "they had problems raising their children. Now the second generation, grown and parents themselves, find it difficult to communicate affection to the third."

Still today the extended family and the parental bonding skills are absent as native teenagers are sent south to begin high school in a distant southern community. They suffer from the disruption of relocation into another culture that often sees them as "different."

The native youth in the southern city or the child on the reserve in a dysfunctional family learns early not to get emotionally close to others, thus has never learned how to positively share feeling of pain, sorrow and loneliness. The child who carries that as rejection of his personhood lacks genuine endorsement for his existence.

"When the pain of his existence becomes overwhelming he strives to escape, using the methods molded by his parents," writes Ivan Doxtator, an Oneida counsellor/teacher. "Through drugs and alcohol he has learned that these alter his emotional and mental state and give him illusions of relief from the agonies of life that help him to cope falsely for brief periods of time."

"When he realizes that these temporary times of escape from the reality of his painful existence have no end in [themselves], he begins to view death as the great escape, as a doorway to a final extinguishing and relieving of his pain. Death therefore is viewed as the final coping action, as the only alternate for possible escape."

I am praying that we will see assembled a mobile crisis compassion team, comprised of dedicated professionals who will respond to these desperate conditions with crisis intervention counselling, and suicide prevention programs.

Early in 1993 when we read of the suicide pact of six native children in Davis Inlet, Labrador. When they were found in an unheated shack, two were already unconscious and the rest violently fought off attempts to save them. What a heartbreaking statement of a demoralized people, that children would seek death rather than life.

Solvent abuse continues to destroy our native children at epidemic levels. A social worker told me that at any given time in Winnipeg, Manitoba, approximately 25 native children can be seen sniffing gas or glue. Jeffrey York, author of The Dispossessed, states, "They begin as young as five years of age...and start dying at age twelve."

As a Native I feel demeaned by these statistics; as a human my heart is sick. As a Christian I have a sense of moral outrage and a conviction that Canada's national conscience must be awakened. The shame of our silence can no longer be hidden. Our north is not strong and it is not free.

"Virtually all aboriginal communities are ticking time bombs which could explode into a wider epidemic of suicide if swift action isn't taken," said George Erasmus, who leads a coalition of Canadian groups.

People are dying. We cannot undo our past actions, but we will be indicted and condemned for our current response. We must accelerate our efforts "to heal the brokenhearted to bring deliverance to the captives and to set at liberty them that are bruised."

Arnold Devlin, a mental health worker in Webequic, a Cree community 500 km north of Thunder Bay, said, "Suicide may be the culmination of the effects of unemployment, lack of education, poverty, overcrowding and the stark contrast between the rich lives Natives see on television and their own desperate conditions."

Ministry Focus to Children

The Native family unit has not decreased in number of children as the non-native home. Jeffrey York writes, "The child per family (in the general population) is one to two children, however the Native family unit has continued to have three to four children."

And yet eight out of ten Native churches are without Sunday Schools. I pray that the Native Children's Ministry Institutes that have been instituted by Spirit Alive TV Ministry will increasingly be held regionally across our nation . Some sample courses are: Parenting and Bonding Skills, Ministry to Children in Crisis and the Establishing of Children's Ministry.

Truly a great ministry to Native Children must be undertaken. Give us more "Jeremiah" that will, "...arise, cry out in the night...pour out their heart like waters before the face of the Lord; lift up thy hand towards him for the life of thy young children." (Lamentations 2:19)

I pray that the desperate act of six Native children will be the Macedonian call from our aboriginal communities that will wake up the church to the developing of trained family ministries.

Natives must not continue to die in the darkness of death at their own hands.

The Bible College Training of Natives

One of the most effective keys to evangelism and long-term church growth is trained Native leadership. Without this, many Natives in churches will continue as group gathering. Bible college trained pastors, through discipleship programs will help to bring structure that will curtail the backsliding of many people.

The lack of indigenous churches has been a great hinderance. On many reserves gathering, called churches, lack proper facilities, have a nurtured dependence and produce little Native leadership. They often do not meet the criteria of being an indigenous church, which is self-governing, self-supporting and self-reproducing.

Let me hasten to say that God is raising up Native Bible colleges that are culturally sensitive with predominantly Native staff. We must be careful that we do not shortchange those that we seek to train with programs that are condensed and on the level of, or beneath that of Sunday School materials.

How often have I seen, to the detriment of the Gospel, Bible Schools for Natives that have come into existence and then failed because proper structure, facilities, finances and faculty have been missing. It has often not been teachers who have taught but individuals that have expressed an interest in Native missions or supporting pastors who could fit a week or two into their schedules.

The training of the Native is essential for reaching his own people. Many denominations implement the indigenous program in missionary endeavors in other nations of the World, which is training the nationals for leadership in the evangelizing of their own people and administration of their own progress. However, in our nation we fail to apply the same principals among the Native people. A partnership of abilities and creative solutions is crucial in reaching Canada's Native population with a gospel of substance and structure.

The Mission Field of the Urban Indian

Another challenge that we face is that the growth rate of the urban Native population and the problems it poses demand that the works of our faith be motivated by the compelling compassion of Christ, who looked over a city and wept.

We in Canada live in a glass house constructed by the media. The shame concerning Canada's Native peoples can no longer be hidden. It has graphically been a front page challenge. Statistics concerning health, housing, poverty, suicide and imprisonment of Natives form an incredible indictment of the failure of programs that have not been creative, credible and consistent in reaching these people. The influx of Natives from economically depressed and suicide plagued reserves is due at least in part to primitive living conditions. Many Natives are tired of two or three families living in the same house, which often lacks modern conveniences.

As a nation we have never faced openly these isolated pockets of poverty and depression. People have lived, and often died untimely deaths, in hidden habitations of cruelty. Now they are coming to the cities; our consciences are being confronted.

In an article entitled, "The Urban Powder Keg" (B.C. Journal, July 13, 1992) Lorner Gunter writes, "The populations of Edmonton, Saskatoon, Regina and Winnipeg are expected to be between 10 percent to 15 percent Native. By the year 2010 the exodus of Indians from remote reserves could increase those percentages by as much as 50 percent."

Most Native leaders, political scientists and statisticians agree that something revolutionary must be done in the Native sectors of our cities. To proceed as before would be both reprehensible and indefensible.

"We have strategized to pierce and plant the gospel among the recently arrived ethnic immigrant groups in our cities," commented Dr. William McRae of Ontario Theological Seminary during the National Days of Prayer for Canadian Indians. "But strangely, we have overlooked the great mission field of the Canadian Indian that is in our midst."

Urban missionaries must be equipped to deal with the problem of inferiority, suicidal tendencies and substance abuse. They must, without prejudice, be able to sympathize with and assist those who have been victimized to the extent that they have lost any hope that their circumstances can be changed.

Above all, urban missionaries must be culturally literate so they will be sensitive. The Native urban immigrants are experiencing traumatic transition; the extended family on the reservation no longer exists. The church must creatively respond to this challenge with new methods of ministry. Prosperous suburban congregations should be partners with existing Native churches in the same city or adjacent reserve.

There must be a mechanism for open communication between Native and non-Native churches. Compassion must be expressed and non-native churches with resources and commitment must respond to the spiritual condition of Natives within the inner cities better than what they did in the past to those who resided in reservations.

New trail blazers, second generation Natives of the cities, are struggling to break new trails that will lead to more meaningful involvement among the religious, political and economical sectors of the urban setting.

I do not see the sun setting on Native Canadian society; in my spirit I see a sunrise and feel a new sense of destiny. I feel the stirring of a hope that "maketh not ashamed," the defusing of the urban Native powder keg in our hands.

A Unified and Empowered Native Leadership

What is needed for a greater in-gathering of a Native harvest is the engendering of unified and empowered Native leadership.

In the history of people denigrated, there comes a time when their cup of endurance is full and threatens to run over. A yearning for change and upward mobility is engulfing Canada's First Nations people. The cry is for leadership and action in the judicial, social, religious, economic and political sectors.

First Nations leaders are struggling to break through oppression that is entrenched by decades of mass generalization and stereotyping of their people, classifying them as drunken, lazy and unprofitable.

There must be a radical overhaul of a governmental system that has positioned Native people at the bottom of every social index.

It is unacceptable that Canada's first peoples, who were here for thousands of years are citizens who cannot use their land as collateral for a loan to ascend out of economic dependency to economic development; citizens who, on average, live 10 years less than other Canadians and whose average income is 36 percent less.

There is a struggle at every level of aboriginal society. An indigenous Native leadership is emerging that no longer wants to remain in subjugation to a system that has paternalized it. It is no longer willing to enforce deliberations and enshrine decrees that have been conceived in some distant office. We need leaders that are culturally sensitive and that will focus on achieving Native solutions to Native problems.

Native leadership is emerging and bridging into the future in the areas of religion, politics and economics. After 400 years of non-Native domination and a denial of cultural distinctiveness, I envision Natives as full participants, not treated as invited guests with observer status. Policies of organization must be inclusive, not exclusive.

In 1992, recognizing that great change was needed, I issued a call for the formation of an evangelical aboriginal think tank. This would be a task force with cultural sensitivity, making submissions to Parliament, the Assembly of First Nations, the news media and religious institutions. Subsequently, they would seek to expedite creative and sensitive outreaches to Native Canadians. The criteria were: that is must be geographically representative, with its members drawn from the political, economic, educational and judicial sectors.

The church is commanded to love her neighbor and to offer a cup of cold water. We together must take the initiative of intercession, evangelism, social action and legislation toward the outcome of a national history that has left a legacy of sorrow.

The Canadian church has placed its mission priority in foreign countries and on distant shores. It needs to become near-sighted and see the tens of thousands of Natives that are filling our cities. Many of these are homeless and churchless. They fill detox and rehab centres, jails and halfway houses, but not our churches. Home missions must be re-examined and their mission strategies must be re-emphasized.

We have strategies to evangelize, penetrate and plant churches within ethnic communities, but strangely we have overlooked a tremendous mission field among us. Either we have overlooked them or stereotyped them as unproductive, unprofitable and unreachable.

The Gospel we preach must not ignore the social dimensions of human well being. We who serve the creator who embraces the pain of all people must not insulate ourselves from the suffering of others.

As Host-Director of the T.V. program called Spirit Alive which is a national Native voice of hope; and President of

National Native Bible College I have witnessed both the frustration and the deep longing for change among Native Canadians. Thank God, today there is a coming together. In June '95 there will be, through the goodwill and sponsorship of both World Vision and the Evangelical Fellowship of Canada, a gathering together of Native delegates to assess the spiritual and physical needs of Native Canada.

This inter-tribal and inter-denominational entity can become perhaps a credible mechanism whereby concerns from mission entities can be submitted to them. This does not presuppose that this is a task force that will have longevity but may be only short-term.

We have survived for a long time, sustained by what some may call "illusions of hope." But today I have great hope for my people, based on the hope and the faith in a great God, a God who can give guidance as old waste places are rebuilt, foundations of many generations are raised up, breaches are repaired and new paths constructed to walk in.

The Involvement of the Non-Native Christian Community

In my capacity as a Native journalist and clergyman, I have often been asked what kind of attitude and support Natives would like to see from the non-Native Christian community. From personal experience and ministry of more than 25 years with my people, I offer the following proposals:

a. Re-emphasize "home missions," with a re-thinking of strategies in light of current statistics pertaining to suicides, hopelessness and imprisonment of Natives.

b. Pray aggressively and compassionately that God will open the eyes and hearts of people to this great mission field; bind the power of Satan and call more workers.

c. Establish, equip and strengthen present Native leadership to be able to stand as role models before their people.

d. Extend full representation for Native people on governing boards - including voting rights and the same financial assistance given to missionaries.

e. Sponsor Native students for study in Bible colleges, and support Native ministries in your mission budgets.

f. Start an operations linkup - where a mother church helps to sponsor another church. Support a struggling evangelical Native church that already exists rather than starting another one on the same reserve.

g. Stop sending well-intentioned but untrained people who have not been educated in cross cultural communications.

h. Listen to the legitimate concerns of Natives without classifying them as rebellious, insubordinate or bitter.

i. Display a sense of confession and humility. The white Christian community has come with an attitude of superiority unconsciously saying, "Be like us and you'll be all right."

j. Establish a branch for Native studies in the missions departments of Bible schools and colleges.

The months ahead present a great challenge concerning the response of the Canadian church to the searching,growth and struggle of the Native people.

I take heart in current endeavors of ministry including: the Commission on First Nation Ministries established by the Baptist Convention of Ontario and Quebec; the annual Native week hosted by 100 Huntley Street; the formation of an Aboriginal Department in World Vision; and the support of many denominations and para-church ministries for the National Day of Prayer for Indians. The focus on native ministry of the 700 Club in Canada in a practical ministry of feeding, and in the creative ministry of counselling and in the convening of an Evangelical Task Force on Aboriginal Concerns.

In Conclusion "Hope deferred maketh the heart sick."
- King Solomon

The path may seem difficult and often hope is crushed, but in my spirit I feel the stirring of a "hope that maketh not ashamed!" Where there has been a deep well of sorrow a mighty river of hope is about to be released. Our Native young people are learning to use the instrument of the white man's success in education and skills - and with those, we shall construct a society that will shatter the barriers of our isolation.

Then, our Native people will have meaningful involvement among the religious, political and economic sectors. Our destiny will not be predetermined by the actions of others. Our dignity no longer denied, our hope no longer deferred. Together, as His children, mutually dependent upon each other, the paths of our minds and will shall merge toward the finding of just solutions.

Canada's reserves need to hear the voice of a praying church above the voice of the religious Native drum. Together as Native and non-Native we must accept the challenge. God has not given the keys of the kingdom to political groups, but rather to the church. May our visions be wide enough to see this neglected mission field in our own homeland and our commitment strong enough to do something about it.

Ross Maracle is a Mohawk Journalist and clergyman, President of National Native Bible College, Deseronto, Ontario and host of television broadcast *Spirit Alive* which is a national Native voice of hope. For further information, contact Ross Maracle, Box 292 Deseronto, Ontario, Canada K0K 1XO

Chapter 10

LOCAL CHURCHES CAN PLANT CROSS-CULTURALLY

Marjorie Osborne

One afternoon in January, 1953, a very unusual event happened. A young man walked into a grade 13 biology class and became the first black person to study in that Toronto high school of 2500. There was no other person in the school who was visibly of a different culture than the rest. Toronto is now proclaimed to be the most multi-cultural city in the world. The south has moved north. The east has moved west and now forty years later, people from all over the globe are here, - not just in the major cities but in the most unexpected corners of this country.

The presence of so many new ethnic groups in Canada alone does not necessitate the church's environment in creating new congregations but one very important factor does. It is the need to worship in the language of the heart.

Unless you have been in a culture so unlike your own that you may have been called with sympathy, `the ignorant one' or tried to worship for months in a language that was not your own you may not yet realize how necessary it is for the spiritual life to find expression in one's mother tongue.

Many local churches are situated close to new populations who need to worship, learn, and evangelize in the language of their hearts. The following are examples of some local churches who decided to make it happen.

New Neighbors Call for a New Vision

Rosewood Church of the Nazarene in Agincourt, Ontario was still a church plant itself when both pastor and people became aware of a major change in the community. It seemed that almost overnight the largely Anglo community had become almost one half Chinese. New people were always in the service but the Chinese were never among those visiting.

Prayerfully the congregation began to plan for the addition of a Chinese congregation. They raised initial support for a pastor's salary and housing and decided they were willing to share facilities. The major concern was, "where would the pastor and Christian nucleus for a church plant be found?"

Through a conversation with the guest speaker at an annual pastors and partners retreat, the pastor heard about an excellent young man studying in Chicago area who had recently come from the Nazarene Church in Hong Kong. He was invited to spend a weekend in Agincourt and in time was asked and agreed to become the church planter for the new Chinese congregation. He needed help. The church supported with prayer, finances, and brochure delivery but no one could speak Cantonese.

On his first Friday of visiting the new church planter met a very cordial Anglo couple who encouraged him to return the next week. They had sold the home to a family from Hong Kong who would be moving in at that time. Imagine the delight of the planter when he returned the next week and found his Christian high school teacher from Hong Kong. He along with his family of five became the support and nucleus of the new congregation. The new family was in touch with a fellow student of the planter's who had also just arrived in Canada. This young man became the first convert. The financial support of the congregation was gradually decreased as the new church was able to look after itself and then take on its share of the facility expenses.

Offer What You Can

In other instances churches have not been able to launch new ethnic congregations with financial support but have been able to offer facilities for worship and fellowship. Often they have been willing to share equipment and provide office space.

Churches can also be spiritual supporters through prayer and encouragement. Joint services of celebration and combined fellowship events benefit all.

Local Anglo churches can also work for the inclusion of new language groups in all denominational functions. This would include translations, participation, and sometimes helping new leaders develop a profile in the denomination. Elections to district and national position depends on the people getting to know new leaders and their skills.

Sometimes Anglo churches can provide support by calling in furlough or retired missionaries within the denomination to facilitate discussions of interest to both congregations or to be a welcomed resource person.

Two churches of the Nazarene in Toronto have really opened their doors in a big way. Kennedy Road Church is used by Anglos, Koreans, Tamils and Nigerians. The Emmanuel Church has Anglo, Spanish, Italian, Tamil and Armenian congregations sharing one facility. The Emmanuel Church also houses "The Toronto Nazarene Bible Institute" which is especially equipped to prepare leaders of ethnic groups for ordination. This is meeting a very real need since often it is a committed, inwardly motivated lay person who is sensing the call of God to gather his or her people together for worship and late became the leader of his Christian ethnic community.

A Vision to Share Rejuvenates

The Grace Church of the Nazarene was a great city church in the 50's but like so many other inner city churches a changing community caught them unaware and serious decline set in. It left them in a state of serious depression with an empty but debt free building by 1988.

Through study of their history and the community they began to feel that God would have them put the building to some good use. God gave a new vision. Once again He was prepared to add to the leaders with vision both resources and people in 1989 `The Sharing Place' opened. Initially it was a place of friendship and counselling for those in need. Food, clothing, and basic housekeeping items were provided.

The first week `The Sharing Place' opened it served eight families. It was hoped by gradually building up resources it would be able to help 60 families a week. Four years later `The Sharing Place' sees around the world. `The Sharing Place' provides immigration and job counselling, ESL classes, literacy classes, head start groups for children, city day camps, nutrition and cooking classes and plenty of friendship opportunities. It has four paid staff and 100 volunteers. You wonder what this has to do with starting new congregations? Spanish, Cambodian, Portuguese, and Slavic congregations and Bible Studies have started as a result. By the way, the original Anglo church is strong, healthy and growing.

Helps For Starting Congregations Cross Culturally

a. Find out who lives in your community.
b. Ask the Lord how your church can meet the need of other language groups.
c. Remember not to confuse `Christianity' with your own or your denomination's cultural baggage.
d. Learn appreciatively from the newcomers.
e. Don't do anything for the new congregation that they could do for themselves.
f. Don't saddle a new congregation with possible future financial hardship. Newcomers may not have much for a long time.
g. Communicate thoroughly.
h. Make careful decisions and inform all congregations about facility use including room and equipment use, cleaning, setting up, signs, damage replacement, etc.
i. Plan in advance so that all congregations understand times and locations of all programs whether held separately or together.
j. Make sure all understand how autonomous each congregation is or will become from the beginning.
k. Be an advocate for the new congregations at all denominational levels and functions.

A Good Difference

Six years ago the Church of the Nazarene in Canada ministered only in English and French. We now have thirty-five churches worshipping in sixteen other languages. The impact of their spiritual vitality is changing us for the better at local, district, and national levels. They are taking responsibility for spreading the gospel among their own language group with excellent results. Their experience, especially in the areas of evangelism and prayer, is motivating our denomination with renewed urgency.

Chapter 11

ISSUES AND CHALLENGES OF INNER-CITY ETHNIC MINISTRIES

Alan Roxburgh

Introduction

The question of issues and challenges facing ethnic ministry in the inner city itself raises questions about the notion of inner city and the language of the ethnic group. There are basic presuppositions which still shape our understanding of the Canadian city and, therefore, the answers to questions about ministry in that setting. The major part of this workshop will address this issue of the way we have conceived the city and the meaning of ministry. This is done on the assumption that these twin perspectives of inner city and ethnic are themselves part of the problem which must be addressed.

The "Inner City," Immigration and Ethnic Groups

What connects these two terms, "inner city" and "ethnic"? The primary connector is immigration. Most groups identified as ethnic came, as minority groups, into Canadian culture as immigrants. Their main entrance point has traditionally been the inner city. While this is no longer the case, the perspective remains a significant interpretive framework within the thinking about immigrant groups.

The inner city, that central core of the old city where the industrial and commercial base was first established, has been the primary point of entrance for immigrant into the city. A brief look at the city like Toronto illustrates this point. Waves of immigrant groups moved through the entry port and settled in the cheap housing and easy laboring, factory jobs of the inner city where many of the earlier industrial base jobs could be found. In the early part of this century, urban theorist began to suggest that the city core was a place of dirt, disease and toil. They argued that the ideal form of city living was an environment incorporating the city into a country-like lifestyle. Consequently the focus of urban life and development shifted. As waves of new immigrant groups entered the city, the more educated, propertied middle classes were establishing homes in corridors along the northern edges of Yonge street laying adjacent to the countryside. It must be remembered that the Don Valley was, in the early part of this century, a demarcation line; to cross the valley was to enter non-urban land. There are still people alive who remember the Danforth, just across from the Don Valley, with wooden side-walks and the city becoming country gardens just one or two blocks north of the Danforth. The new immigrants initially moved into those urban areas vacated by more established, usually Anglo, groups heading out to new homes. This became a massive movement to suburbanization following World War II, but all the seeds for that shift had been planted and were developing from early in the century.

The new immigrant groups settled in the inner core, established themselves, built communities and had families. Often, by the second and third generations, there was then a new movement as the children of the original immigrants joined the more pervasive flow of population out into the growing suburbs. An example of this movement would be in the west-end of Toronto in a section known as little Portugal. Originally a blue collar, Anglo dominated community it became the entry point for Portuguese speaking people from Portugal, the Azores and Brazil. As Anglos moved north and west into newer suburban areas, the Portuguese language came to characterize the area. Religiously, these people groups were tightly knit social groupings with strong cultural ties to the Roman Catholic church. They may not have been deeply devout Catholics but their catholicity was an integral element in their cultural identity. This, of course, made it extremely difficult for first and second generations to cross any religious barriers. But as the second and third generations emerged, moved through the dominant culture school system, they acculturated into the larger society and moved to the suburbs. While new Portuguese immigrants continue to enter the original points of entrance in the downtown of west Toronto, it has now also become the entrance point for even more recent people groups. Vietnamese groups now become a visible part of the social mix in this entry point, transition neighborhood. It is this type of people movement which identifies so called ethnics in the inner city.

What I want to pick up at this point is the nature of these immigrants and how they fit into the economic development of the city. Traditionally, in modern cities, immigration has been linked with industrialization and certain kinds of economic development. Ethnic minorities have, typically, provided the human resource base for the industrialization and construction which went into urban expansion. Usually, the job skills were in the building trades, low skills industrial work and service sector work. This process can be recognized in Western Europe, especially France and Germany, where large numbers of ethnic minorities from Africa and Asia have immigrated to fill in the industrial work needs of a more educated and affluent national population. A similar pattern is observed in Hong Kong where young Filipinos work as cleaners and child care workers for the affluent Chinese populations. In most cases the inner core of the cities provides the host areas for such people groups.

In Western countries there is now an uncoupling of these long established immigration patterns linking industrialization and immigration. We have experienced a massive de-industrialization of urban cores. This economic transition not only creates high levels of unemployment among low paid and unskilled workers but also breaks the traditional patterns of immigration. This has resulted in the emergence of critical issues which must be addressed before effective ministry among ethnic groups entering the country is possible. The following is a brief list of these issues:

a. The disappearance of traditional employment sources for ethnic immigrants.

b. The growing levels of reaction toward minority groups within the cities. This is illustrated in both the harsh immigration policies of certain right of centre parties as well as increased racial tensions among groups in the city.

c. More fundamental questions about immigration policy are being raised. The Globe and Mail (Saturday, April 25, 1993, p.1) discussed the social cost of immigration on institutions such as schools and asked if current immigration policy actually serves the function for which it was created, namely, the supply of people for the labour market in an industrialized society.

What lies ahead then, is a very different set of variables shaping the types of ethnic groups who enter the Canadian city. Along with this is the question of whether it can really be maintained that there is, in fact, a Canadian stereotype called the inner city where ethnic immigrant groups come to establish their initial communities. Certainly, in the case of groups like the Chinese, Iranians and those from Korea, these stereotypes no longer apply.

Religious Institutions and Ethnic Movement in the "Inner City"

As this long term process continued, the religious institutions also underwent significant transformation. Initially, the strong dominant culture churches acted as advocates and sources of assistance for the immigrant groups. The churches provided not only food and shelter but education and transition training. But, as the dominant culture groups moved up the socio-economic pyramid, taking their new status out to the suburbs, these relationships slowly changed. While people moved to new neighborhoods, more homogeneous and comprised of their own topologies, they continued returning to their church buildings in the old neighborhoods of parents and grandparents. These churches continued as central meeting points and symbols of history, tradition and identity even while the neighborhoods themselves changed dramatically. In time the number of people returning to the original church for ongoing sustenance and identity dwindled. This meant, for example, that for Anglo churches in these neighborhoods there was significant decline. Churches became warehouses for small, aging groups of people clinging to their past and longing for a time when the large communities of social faith they had once experienced would return. The new immigrant groups were increasingly viewed as aliens, strange interlopers who had moved into the old neighborhood, destroying its character.

Changing Ethnic Groups

A change in the type of ethnic groups entering the city also needs to be addressed. Statistics show that immigrants tend to live in urban areas. Toronto is city with a large ethnic population and a high degree of ethnic diversity. Immigration alone accounts for 38% of its population. One of the fundamental changes in the patterns of immigration has been the source countries. Today, over 50 per cent of immigrants to Toronto come from Asia and the Middle East. This requires a dramatic shift in perspective and strategy among those seeking to establish ministries among these new populations. In the recent past, immigrants have come from people groups representing Europe and South America who bring with them some rooting in a broadly Christian tradition. This has made the tradition issues in terms of cross-cultural communication a relatively manageable issue. In such cases, the dominant culture has seen mission as a matter of understanding how to convince "ethnic" groups to cross socio-cultural boundaries within a broadly Christian tradition. In a sense, people were being asked to switch from one brand of apples to another.

The context we face today is radically different. We are now looking at the question of how to change people groups who come from outside the Christian tradition. Further more, these people groups are often not comprised of the older industrial worker with low level skills in need of basic assistance in getting established. The new immigrant is in a far different position. This "ethnic" grouping, coupled with the rapid re-gentrification of so called inner cities, requires a radical rethinking of our missionary theology for the urban centres.

The "Inner City"

The last point brings us back to the notion of the "inner city". The meaning of this phrase needs to be carefully unpacked. While many may disagree, I would argue that this term is more at home in the U.S. than Canadian. This is not to deny the existence of poverty in the urban cores, but the notion of inner city has some clear, identifiable characteristics. Using this label may not be helpful in shaping a strategy for reaching new people groups in the core centres of our cities. Ray Bakke, in his book *The Urban Christian*, identifies this concept as the city core areas which have been abandoned by the white middle class' flight to the suburbs. The inner city areas are then declined economically and peopled by minority groups who cannot afford, socially and educationally, to make the suburban transition. From this perspective, the inner city is perceived by the churches as a place of threat and fear, an economic mission zone. While there is some evidence of this in Canadian cities, it does not describe the nature of the city centres in this country. The term "city core" is more useful than "inner city" for the Canadian setting. The city core is characterized by economic rejuvenation, a multiplicity of people and socio-economic groups. The cores of Canadian cities have been largely places of dynamic economic and cultural inter-mixing over the past several decades. This fact should shape any discussion of ministry across cultural boundaries in our city centres.

The "Ethnic" in Ethnic Ministry

It is important to address the way in which we use language. The term "ethnic" has been traditionally used to describe the kind of ministry which is done with and for newer, immigrant peoples. The term has several meanings. Generally, it is used to describe minority groups whose language, identity and customs differ significantly from the dominant cultural grouping. One of the basic challenges facing ministry in a multi-cultural setting is that of overcoming the presuppositions which lie behind the use of this word "ethnic." It is a word of power. Notions of racial superiority are latent in its use. The need to address our presuppositions are particularly urgent in the light of demographic changes in Canadian cities away from the older, dominant Euro-Christian groupings to the Afro-Asian groupings which are decidedly non-Christian in character. A fundamental barrier to the emergence of much needed new strategies in missional engagement within the complex, multi-cultural character of Canadian cities is the ethnocentrism and latent racism inherent in many of our assumptions about how culture works and what ministry means among immigrant groups in the city. The term ethnic harbors a paternalistic response by dominant cultures to these newly arriving peoples of differing cultural backgrounds. It often carries the assumption that these peoples will become Christians in essentially the same way as the dominant culture; its just that the language and customs will be different for a while, but eventually there will be a blending into the pervasive culture.

Examples of this problematic use of the term "ethnic" are numerous. A vibrant Portuguese congregation in the city core developed within a church building, owned by an Anglo group. The once dominant Anglo culture has been dwindling for some thirty years. They can no longer manage the cost and upkeep of building or pastoral staff. They are aware that their once Anglo community has been changing rapidly as the new ethnics move in, buying up houses left vacant by Anglos moving to the suburbs. There are no longer any new families to keep the church growing. The congregation is aging and is stuck in a form of worship and organizational polity shaped when they were young and the church was vibrant. They want their church to remain active in the community because it keeps alive their memory of what the neighborhood once represented. Their fervent hope and prayer is that someday, somehow, their church could be returned to its former state, filled with vibrant young people running church programmes shaped by the ethos of the fifties.

But they sense that unless dramatic action is taken, the church's doors will have to close. They decide that the best way to deal with these issues is by initiating an "ethnic" ministry to the Portuguese speaking immigrants now populating the community. Their denomination has also decided that ethnic ministry must become a priority and are looking for urban centre churches which will enter into this new venture for ministry and mission. So a dying congregation of aging Anglo Christians who want to keep their church in the community is linked with a new denominational programme for reaching the ethnic groups now entering the city. The denomination provides the funds to hire a Portuguese pastor for the congregation to work alongside the Anglo pastor. And so begins a strategy to reach the ethnics in the community. As a Portuguese congregation develops so do the stress points between the ethnics and the Anglos. "Our" church is getting very messy, they complain. These ethnics don't clean up after themselves. The smell of their strange foods lingers on in the building after they have had their Sunday lunches. It is just too much. These feelings hardly ever get expressed in a forum where cross-cultural issues can be heard and addressed because that was never the actual basis for the initial ministry from the perspective of the host church. Ethnic ministry was a survival tactic for the church and a way of doing something in a rapidly changing community. It was always assumed that the Anglo group would remain dominant. It was their church, the Portuguese were guests in the building. The way these issues are worked through are in terms of power issues. Who has control of the building, compelling the "ethnic" group to live by the constitution and by-laws of the church even though these were written for a turn-of-the-century Anglo culture and had little fit for the new people groups whose life was expressed in different cultural forms.

A similar story could be told in another part of the city centre. Again, a declining Anglo congregation inhabiting a main street church building with a long history and deep set of traditions looks out at its community, lamenting the massive changes that have taken place. Their once tranquil neighborhood is now the home of new people group whose sights, sounds and smiles are alien to the church group who once dominated the neighborhood. As in the previous case, the church and the denomination decided that the way into the future was to develop an "ethnic" ministry for the church. The result was almost identical. Hispanic and black groups were invited into the church but their music and language immediately become problematic. The Anglo congregation, now less than forty people, insisted that it remain in the main sanctuary even though the other groups had become much larger. The tensions were played out through familiar power games concerning who owned the building and who had the right to make the final decisions about pastoral leadership and strategies for ministry. Only when the church was closed down and the aging Anglo group finally agreed to relinquish their church was it possible to initiate vital congregations, comprised of various people groups using the same buildings.

Behind each of these illustrations lies the notion that "ethnic" ministry is a certain form of dominant culture outreach to those who will, sooner or latter, assimilate into the broader cultures and become Christian, in a way similar to the dominant group. In the multi-cultural urban centres of Canada this will no longer be the case. Thus a radically different way of thinking about ministry is required in this new context. We can no longer be shaped by a colonial approach to mission in the urban world. This will be a painful and difficult transition for many of those who have long enjoyed places of dominance and control within church systems. The Council of Jerusalem, recorded in the Book of Acts is paradigmatic for our context. It reflects the basic issues which we must face in our cities if there is to be an adequate response to the challenges before us. At Jerusalem there was a significant movement of the Spirit in which culturally narrow and ethnocentric Christian leaders were able to free the Gospel to take the form and shape required to speak meaningfully into another culture. The missional ecclesiology, no people-group should be required to conform to a perceived dominant culture for salvation, was decided at this council for
the Gospel was not to be monopolized by any dominant social group.

Therefore, a genuinely new form of church required for the cities of our day will not be one which simply provides a building in which different people groups are warehoused under the control of a dominant group nor of a worship service comprised of differing nationalities but English hymns and the organ dominate. It will be a church in which the unique cultural forms of a group are celebrated and set free as a genuine form of Gospel wineskin for that neighborhood. The challenge of inner city, ethnic ministry is to fundamentally redefine these categories because: firstly, they do not describe the reality of the Canadian city and; secondly, they represent presuppositions which form significant barriers to ministry in the city.

While these remain the primary questions for ministry in the urban core churches, there are a second level of questions that need to be addressed in the formation of new strategies for ministry in the multi-form city of today.

a. Host congregations must be helped to work through their issues of power and identity.

b. Funding remains a massive problem which will only get worse as denominations continue to lose their funding basis. The resources to do effective urban missiology require long term funding. New congregations may take a long time in becoming self supporting. How funds can be found for the long term commitments required is an extremely difficult issue in a period of major retrenchment among denominations.

c. Issues of cultural dislocation must be addressed. Neither home of origin nor new home provides a place of settledness for some first generation groups. They become an in-between people yearning for the old customs and unable to embrace the new realities. In some cases, such groups become lost, with no place of their own. They represent a great challenge to cross-cultural ministry.

d. Pastoral training for the modern city continues to remain one of the primary areas seminaries have yet to address. Leadership and care models among the newer people groups often do not function in the classic Western styles of pastoral ministry or theological education.

e. Many new, city core churches may be congregations which meet in a downtown building but the people themselves are actually spread across wide areas of the city. It is difficult to continue the social bonding and community so central to their lives. This kind of dislocation creates significant problem in terms of the groups self identity and social cohesion. Modern cities function around social sub-groups rather than family centres. The fragmenting and individualizing pressures of the modern city require careful strategizing for ministry among the new immigrant groups.

f. Work patterns become disruptive of traditional church models. Often the immigrant groups, even though highly skilled in their home country, find themselves in low paying, maintenance jobs outside their fields. Night shifts, learning to function in the twenty-four hour city, work below levels of competency or long periods of unemployment not only affect self-esteem but break the traditional bonds brought from the country of origin.

g. How are the leaders of these new immigrant churches empowered to take leadership and re-shape the forms and structures of denominations and local judicatories? If this basic unit of socio-cultural organization does not change dramatically the newer leaders will still feel a colonializing and paternalistic attitude from these larger groups. In the city, these units of organization will need to be completely re-designed before a more comprehensive urban strategy can take shape. Such redesigning cannot be done from the top down but grow out of grassroots organization and planning in which the newer groupings are invited to the table as equals.

Chapter 12

USING STATISTICS AND STRATEGIES IN ETHNIC CHURCH PLANTING

Brian Seim & Wencesloa Garcia

Okay, I'm just sitting here looking at this list of words and numbers. They told me that this would be useful as I begin to think about my new church plant. What they forgot to tell me was how it might be useful. They also forgot to tell me that I'd need to get some bifocals to read all those little columns and lines. Yep, here I am! And I could have gone to my church building maintenance meeting instead.

Perhaps like the church planter above, demographics have never made it across your desk without you falling asleep. However, when Census Canada makes their study every five years, they ask some very practical questions. Marketing firms spend thousands of dollars on that data and city halls are crying for the information long before it's ready to make sure they are serving the people they think they are serving.

So it must be useful. But how? And where on earth do I get my hands on it?

In an urban center you can go to the nearest research library (usually the main branch) and copy the material from the four census tracts closest to your intended area of ministry. Every census tract in Canada has material available on its population, gender and age, mother tongue and place of birth. It will tell you when people entered Canada and how many immigrants of that background are in each census tract. If you look at the larger guide to that community you will see their occupation and educational background.

But the key to evaluating anything is asking the right questions. In strategizing for ethnic church planting there are several sets of questions you need to ask. The two most important sets of question are directed to government and other churches in the community. But right now it's time to take a pad of paper down to the library, find the most comfortable chair in the place (because you're going to be there for awhile and ask yourself some questions).

Key Information That I could derive from the Census Data

Population - Who Is Coming to my Doorstep?

Did you know that the population of Toronto increased by 13.6% over the last five years. Did you know that Vancouver had a 16.1% increase over the same period? Edmonton, Calgary and the Cambridge-Kitchener-Waterloo area are growing at between 8-15% as well. Much of that growth is from newcomers to Canada.

How many people of your Target Group arrived in the last five years? Is this number growing? How do new immigrants feel as they first encounter these North American cities and then see them change so quickly? How can you as a church help them with these drastic changes? When new Canadians arrive, many cast off their spiritual authority. Whether they come from Muslim, Hindu, Buddhist or even Christian background, they are open to anything within our culture that meets their needs. Meeting people's felt needs with loving care opens doors to their real need, Jesus Christ! Within 18 months of arrival, immigrants are settled into their new lifestyle and value system.

Gender and Age - How Do You Reach The Individual In This Group?

Knowing the age and sex of your target group determines what kind of outreach you will use. Do I need a new mother's ministry, a single men's sports program, a nannie's tea or a lunch twice a week for retirees?

Mother Tongue - How Much Has Your Target Group Acculturated?

Do the people I wish to reach still feel a strong affinity for the language of their homeland or just for the culture? Do we need an English language service for the children? Wherever I speak at an ethnic church that has been established more than ten years, this is the first question that comes up, both from the leadership and from among the youth.

Date of Immigration and Citizenship - When Did They Arrive?

Are they still in culture shock? Have they, as a group become successful here or has it been a difficult time for them?

What sub-groups of culture do you have in your target group? Two Sri Lankan friends illustrate this well. One arrived in 1974 as a graduate student and is a successful research engineer today. The other taught university in Sri Lanka until 1988 and escaped the country with only his life when he was identified with a dissident group. Today he is a janitor. These subgroups need to be identified and their needs evaluated separately - then together. If a key leader of your work arrived under extreme circumstances, it is wise to draw in others around him who do not react the same way so that they can filter these intense thoughts and opinions.

Most immigrants become Canadian citizens within seven years. That may signal a desire for acculturation, a means of bringing over family, an ascension of power, an ownership of their new land. What do these things mean in your culture group?

Dwelling and Household Characteristics - Where Do Your People Live?

It's time to get out your map! People live in a time/space relationship. If many people travel an hour and a half by bus each way to work how will it affect their church attendance if we meet an hour away? What does the map tell me about my area of the city? Is my site accessible to the people I want to reach? Can my people reach it by bus, street-cars, highways driving? Does the target group have access to cars? How far will they travel? An experienced church planting friend started a church among his own people alongside a willing English congregation and ended up with very erratic attendance because the buses only came within five blocks of the church.

Living Arrangement, Marital Status & Family - How Do Your People Live?

Are they sharing apartments with others? Is that putting special peer pressures on them which affect their Christian walk? Is there a high incidence of single mothers in my target neighborhood? How can I meet the needs of these women? How are non-family units viewed in my culture and what do I need to do to minister effectively to these singles?

Ordinarily, singles and couples without children are members in an ethnic group first to arrive in Canada. A young man arrived from Singapore with a M.B.A and spent nearly 18 months trying to find a job. He desperately needed the sports ministry he got involved in. A ministry to this target group is quite different from the other one serving an established immigrant group with families.

Income, Job and Education - How Is Your Target Group's Self- Image?

Immigrants usually start out with a very strong self-image and primary providers are not accepted for immigration into Canada unless they are expected to make a significant contribution to this society. But what is significant to the Canadian Government may not be significant to a new immigrant.

Have the people in your focus group, in their own minds, accomplished their potential? What kind of atmosphere do they prefer to walk into that would make them feel at home? What secondary interest (sports, hobbies, important non-religious holidays) do these people have?

Key Questions for My Church Planting Team:

In What Areas Do You Need Help in Leadership?

Do Christian leaders already exist in my people group? What are their three greatest areas of need in training? What areas are they qualified to teach me in? Are they involved in outreach and if so what are the results? How can I, through the new outreach, develop the spiritual gifts and leadership of my church planting team? What parts of the training should be done through systematic leadership training in the context of an accountability group? Would it help me to team up with a mission agency located in my area to add to manpower and help train secondary leadership? Are there weaknesses in my church planting team caused by sin and moral issues which need to be taken care of before we begin to share Christ with others?

Language

It is right and valuable to worship in our mother tongue, but how can we keep it from being a platform for prejudice? There are Anglo churches that will only use the King James Version of the Bible. In other cultures, their language has become the only "Holy Language", the way to approach God. God is not that small. He made that clear at Pentecost. He loves us all as well as our languages. What can I put into our long term plan that will help us make wise decisions when our children want to worship in their heart language?

The curse of Babel is real in our natural selves and all of us have prejudice in our hearts. But the power to overcome it is real as well. We are reminded many times in the New Testament that Christ has broken down the barriers and in Him there is no barriers because of ethnicity. Prejudice is a sin just like any other sin. We have the capability to overcome sin through the empowerment of the Holy Spirit. He uses relationships (more than one) to break down prejudice. How can I facilitate this kind of change for my people?

In 1985 I took a group of college and career students to the middle of the Amazon to show the "Jesus Film". One of the women became very good friends with the Brazilian Indian woman. I used to marvel as they walked down the road laughing at a dozen things and separated only by the fact that neither spoke a word of the other's language. God can break down even language barriers!

What Human Elements Help People to Respond to the Gospel?

People come to the Lord from a human point of view out of a concentration of prayer, understanding, and relationship.

Prayer helps us to determine that God's interest is the same as ours. He responds by bringing people to you who already have a desire for Him. Concentrated frequent prayer yields a refined plan, a unity with others in similar ministry and an excellence in ministry.

Understanding includes a clear mental comprehension of the gospel, an ability to socially integrate that knowledge and finally a personal commitment to the knowledge. For example, older adults usually have no problem with their mental understanding. They may have some reservations about life style changes. But once the commitment is made at that age, it is much less likely to change.

Relationships are the goal of every activity: sports leagues, Sunday schools, even worship is aimed at developing relationships. Some of these relationships are with the Lord and some are with people. Activities show onlookers an integrated lifestyle and when our lives are integrated with the Lord they attract people to Him.

So we put prayer, understanding and relationship into every ministry equation and it yields a fruitful harvest.

Spiritual Resistance

What religions are part of the background of your people group? What prayer initiatives need to be made in order to penetrate these religions? What folk ideologies exist in your homeland? Here in Canada? How much of it lies within the occult? Increasingly, I find myself receiving a night phone call from a person going through real spiritual oppression and needing help. I am very careful what I call oppression, but it is clear that when a person has been exposed to the occult and has become attached through someone else's dedication of them or through their own commitment to the occult. When they become serious about Christ, there's going to be a battle. Am I trusting God to overcome the evil one?

Will We Be Mono-Cultural, Multi-Ethnic Or Multi-Congregational?

Mono-cultural churches have one primary culture from which all cultural decisions and theological interpretations emanate. Multi-cultural churches have a commitment to leadership and interpretation from many cultures within one congregation. The Multi-congregational church has several congregations made up of different ethnic groups, but the leadership of each of the congregations makes up one church.

One of the great challenges that face ethnic church plants is the question of how to form a viable church. In the case of people coming from countries with a smaller population here in Canada there are some choices to make. Some of the questions helpful in making these choices necessary are: how do we get a facility, keep part or full-time help paid and make sure we have a church that runs smoothly? How do we bring our youth to love God in the wisest way? Each of these three models has strengths and weaknesses in these regards.

Mono-Cultural

The pluses for a mono-cultural church are many. First, culture and language are a great determiner of like-mindedness. Second, friendships developed within the same culture have a better chance of being understood and are not as emotionally draining, therefore the Gospel comes across much better. If outreach to their own people group remains a primary focus of the mono-cultural church (and that focus is realistic), then it is a true expression of body life. Otherwise, it can easily become a club or a racial statement, excluding both the non-Christian and Christians from other ethnic backgrounds.

The single language church and the multi-cultural church are usually one and the same. To have a Hispanic church today in Canada that only has one nation group in it is almost unheard of. Across Canada I can't think of any Chinese churches that do not have several cultures. There are a few mono-cultural churches left; Filipino, English (the country), Jamaican, German, Laos, and my of the outreaches to the North Indian sub-continent.

The Multi-Cultural Church

The second option available is a decision for a multi-cultural church. This is a single language church that is made up of many cultures. Those cultures could be broken down into socio-economic classes, country groups or dialect groups. To be workable they need leaders from each culture within the full church leadership, a wise, senior leader with a great deal of integrity to lead them, and an open door to hear issues and work out relationships. There also needs to be a commitment to unleashing leaders into leadership, especially among the youth. This is the way it was in the original churches of Jerusalem and Antioch, macro-managing direction and purpose and micro-managing personal issues.

The Multi-congregational Church

The third kind of church government is a multi-congregational church. In this church, there must be real respect across cultures at the leadership level. Again there needs to be representative leadership but the leaders now take on the full role of a pastor or congregational leader themselves. Therefore the senior mentoring pastor must be even more flexible and allow greater autonomy.

The youth in a multi-congregational church have the opportunity to meet together which in the next generation is going to help the rest of the church. It is possible to have a building of your own with this model even with a smaller congregational population. New works can begin out of this model because it is designed to accept new cultures.

The work begins by discipling potential leaders (lots of them) from an incoming ethnic group. As these leaders are developed they can focus on meeting the felt needs of their particular group. Any true mentoring system includes an evaluation of development and that development must be in the context of ministry. By training through ministry, successes yield future potential and failures are really a part of the training and should not determine future ministry among that people group.

One church in San Diego has grown three more congregations of 100 to 300 people by using the three stages listed below to precede full deployment of a congregation. The potential leader is:

a. responsible for a cell group (4-5 people)

b. acknowledged by the church of the growth of cell into a ministry (12 people with an outreach strategy)

c. acknowledged by the mother church of a graduation from a ministry into a congregation (leadership team of 4 - 5, group of 30 with their own master plan for growth)

One final question: What do I want this church to look like in two years, five years, ten years? Now relax, you're ready to get together with your team and ask them some questions.

Evaluation is the first stage of strategy but left there, nothing will happen. Your church planting team is made up of individuals, each coming into this effort with expectations and hopes. God has given each of you different gifts which may look to be opposition at times if there is no clarification.

To facilitate this stage of key communication and planning I would like to suggest "The Church Planting Workbook" by Logan & Rast (Charles E. Fuller Institute of Evangelism and Church Growth, 1985). It has some of the best planning material available. On pages 49-56 is a comprehensive planning guide that will help clarify and solidify your effort. Schedule at least three or four sessions to complete this philosophy of ministry study which is done together in your leadership group. The whole book is a valuable resource in several other ways as far as check lists, priority lists and ideas are concerned.

Following evaluation and planning, you are ready to attempt your church plant. Now you know your community, your needs, your precess, your resources and your goal. Prayerfully, you are seated deeply in God's matchless and endless resources. Now you know better the patient process to which you are to lay your hand and expecting what is to come, discouragement and frustration can readily be brought back to the Cross. You have evaluated the spiritual forces that battle in the community which you have targeted, and with the Amour of God and the Sword of the Spirit, you are ready to take action against them. Demographics don't solve all our problems, but often the most successful leaders are not those who have all the answers, but rather those who have asked the right questions.

Chapter 13

WHAT DENOMINATIONAL LEADERS SHOULD KNOW BUT HAVE NEVER BEEN TOLDREGARDING INTERCULTURAL MINISTRIES

T.V. Thomas[1] & Enoch Wan[2]

Introduction

Personal Information

The presenters of this workshop have been involved in ethnic ministries in Asia and North America. Being of Chinese and Indian/Malaysian descents, we have worked with Caucasians in denominational and trans-denominational contexts at local and national levels. The content of this workshop is based on personal experience and co-operative research.

Purposes/Objectives of the Workshop

This workshop is conducted for the purpose of providing "North American Caucasian" (NAC) denominational leaders with information and insights into what they need to hear from their ethnic (i.e. non-Caucasian) co-workers but have never been told.

Research Methodology (see separate questionnaire)

A questionnaire (see Appendix) with fifteen open-ended questions was designed and distributed to dozens of ethnic workers for their in-put. The presenters then incorporated the result of the survey into this ethnographic[3] study presented here from an "emic"[4] perspective.

Personnel

An ethnic worker is trained in his own cultural context to conform and comply to the "group" which is the core of decision and judgement for its members (see Table 1). When coming into contact with the Caucasian "self" at the beginning stage of intercultural interaction, he may find it enviable to have the freedom and be **fascinated** by the type of self-determination and self-confidence a Caucasian "self" can enjoy. However, upon closer examination and longer interaction, he may be **frustrated** and later find it offensive. Unless he is allowed and wants to assimilate into the Caucasian way, he will **flee** from the "egoistic Caucasian" and isolate himself from further interaction or run the "risk" of being assimilated to the "undesirable" trait (according to his own cultural heritage). He may want to **fight** against Caucasian influence and **find** ethnic identity and psychological security by retreating to interact with members of similar ethnic background only (some would call this "ghetto" mentality). His own cultural up-bringing will prohibit him from being **frank** to the Caucasian about his own negative feeling and **forthright** of his criticism of the Caucasian way. Consequently, there are things that denominational leaders should know but have never been told from an "emic" perspective regarding intercultural ministry.

An ethnic worker (including most of those from European cultures) is generally required to use the formal way to address his colleagues, especially his superior and members of the opposite sex. He feels very uncomfortable when a NAC calls him by his first name. When NACs insisted on him to conform to the first-name basis of address, he feels uneasy and awkward. It would be worse if his NAC superior is the one insisting it. According to his own cultural norm, he should follow the instruction of his superior. Yet he finds it habitually hard to change to the NAC way and personally he is afraid that his peers will accuse him of being disrespectful to his superior, a terrible misconduct of a "spiritual servant" in the ministry.

Occasionally, when the first lady of the denomination happens to be dressing casually, laughing out heartily and loudly, cracking jokes informally, the ethnic worker will find that to be very unbecoming and embarrassing.

An ethnic worker is most grateful to the many kind deeds of NAC colleagues toward him and his family, as in the case of newly arrived Vietnamese pastor from a refugee camp. He surely can use the financial and material assistance provided by NAC. However, at the same time he feels being trapped to become a "bond servant" with a life-time obligation to pay back his indebtedness to the NAC. Later when he sees the blatant cultural misconduct of NAC within the context of Vietnamese community, he would not dare to tell the NAC the truth to help prevent future major blunder the NAC may later commit. When the NAC had done something grossly wrong in the Vietnamese context, the NAC would blame the Vietnamese pastor for not telling the truth. (See **Table 1**)

Policy

Several illustrations from **Table 2** will be selectively presented in terms of "policy."

The rolicy of leadership selection differs among NAC is very different from that of other ethnic groups. NACs usually operate on objective criteria in the selection and promotion of leaders, such as academic qualification, success in membership growth and budgetary increase. Ethnic ways are less scientific: personal and spiritual character, relational skill, personal integrity and reputation. Similarly, ethnic workers tend to place more focus on the intangible way of reward such as honor and shame.

Ethnic workers cannot understand and will not readily conform to the NAC's insistence/ practice of the use of structured meeting, scheduled appointment, specific job description, detailed programming and budgeting, setting short- and long-term goals, etc. They see that as the way of the world thus "unspiritual." They think **pastoring** (or any other form of Christian ministry) is like **parenting**: spontaneous, intensive, personal, informal and unstructured. They despise the NAC's way as merely "professional" and not spiritual.

Professionalism in ministry is deemed by ethnic workers as conforming to the world, and degrading to impersonal enterprising. They decry NAC's emphasis on "doing" as no more like "Martha's busy **doing for the Lord**" and they desire "Mary's service of "**being with the Lord**." Compartmentalizing life to "**profession** in ministry" and "privatize **personal** life" is regarded as hypocritical and Pharisaic. There is the priority of a person's character over career, personhood over performance/productivity, relation over function, godliness/ graciousness over giftedness, etc; yet they insist on the **unity** of these qualities.

Table 1 - THINGS RELATED TO PERSONNEL

AREA	CAUCASIAN: *PERCEPTION/ CONCEPTION/ OPERATION*	NON-CAUCASIAN *FASCINATION/FRUSTRATION*
PERSONAL	"self" : the core of decision & judgement	"Caucasian 'self' provides freedom but is childish & narcissist"
	individualism	fascinated by the oppt. to be free from pressure to conform & comply in the old way
	"group" : perceived as a collection of individuals	individuality & strength found in group
INTERPERSONAL	informality & friendliness	friendship helpful in coping with loneliness in a strange land yet feel uncomfortable with too much informality
	egalitarian	hierarchy & status should be kept
	expressive & direct	seemed too childish & rude
	benevolent, kind & caring	appreciated but fearful to be indebted and later can't reciprocate
	"west is the best"	feels inferior when encountering ethnocentrism or laments "racism"
PROFESSIONAL	professional & not to be personal	cold & impersonal; disregard personal ties/feeling
	emphasizes giftedness & specialization	too "worldly" and secular

The focus of this discussion is not on which orientation or mentality is more scriptural/spiritual. It only describes the differences between the two systems and reports the opinion and sentiment from the ethnic worker's perspective.

Table 2 - THINGS RELATED TO POLICY

AREA	CAUCASIAN *CONCEPTION/ PERCEPTION/ OPERATION*	NON-CAUCASIAN *FASCINATION/FRUSTRATION*
LEADERSHIP	defined by objective criteria	defined by non-quantifiable criteria
	earn by productivity; promotion according to performance	ascribed regardless of performance or productivity
	"he who foots the bill has the most say"	"He who is older/wiser has the most say"
RULES	good & desirable, e.g. "conflict of interest" guideline	too restrictive; flexibility accorded to privileged individuals & circumstances
	ruled by majority democratically with open debate	ruled by consensus in hierarchical system; prefer dialogue and discussion
REWARD	to success: based on productivity & performance	to those who are good at SIR "smooth inter-personal relationship"
	in tangible way	intangible ways: positive - honor, negative - shame

ADMINISTRATION & OPERATION	departmentalize congregation & denomination.	nurturing solidarity of group (e.g. family & kin) by group activity
	compartmentalize life into public & private, professional & personal	fusing of public & private, personal & professional, aspects of life
	prefer pragmatic ("how to"): doing, program	prefer politics ("with Whom"): being & people,
	encourage competition leading to improvement & progress	competition strains relationship, causes conflict & loss of face; should be replaced by cooperation
	time-orientation for punctuality & program	event-orientation when the right people are all there; no event should be ruled by the clock
	planning & programming with measurable goal, quantifiable results, structured activity, job description, budget, etc.	"planning & programming are unspiritual & worldly; play by ear and just let things be"
	"loyalty to my organization supersedes personal ties"	"loyalty to my family & friend; rules & regulations are too restrictive"
	"if I can make the most impact & contribute to change, believe **me**, I will do it"	"if a denomination can get you for cheap, believe me, they will do it"
	"progressive reduction scale in subsidy will lead to desirable self-reliance"	"it should not be imposed uniformly; pending on the individuals involved and the circumstances"
	"ethnics (Asians & Haitians, etc.) are all alike and all rules are applicable to all of them"	"can't they see that North Vietnamese are different from South Vietnamese?" "I am not Japanese; I am Chinese"
	"he who foots the bill has the most say"	"he who is male/old/leader has the most say"

Process

In the process of intercultural ministry, ethnic workers with non-Christian background tend to treasure the shared Christian identity with ethnic co-workers, even those of a different denomination. In the process of interacting with ethnic co-workers of other denominations, they find the old cultural identity and the new found Christian identity ("the new self") to be stronger and more important than that of denomination's (NAC's "us" in terms of voluntary/contractual denominational ties). Thus they feel the denominational leader/administrator to be parochially too denominational.

Their attitude/sentiment is similar to that of the overseas missionaries who are happy to work closely with fellow missionaries of other mission boards or denominations, especially with those who come from the same country/culture or speak the same language. They also see the insistence of mission administrator on denominational demarcation or division to be arbitrary and unspiritual.

In the process of intercultural ministry, ethnic workers have much hesitation in conforming to the NAC's orientation towards task, time, efforts, efficiency and change (see **Table 3** below). These cultural traits are not shared by ethnic workers who do not have the background in the cultural history of technological revolution, Protestant/puritan ethic, frontier development, etc. They may not feel comfortable to be expressively critical of the NAC's way of operating, the

NAC denominational leaders should know the difference and appreciate their apprehension to change and the apathy to the NAC's challenge to be "fruitful" (re: "productive," "efficient") for the Lord.

During the process of interacting with one and other, ethnic workers take the NAC's every move personally and in the wrong way, e.g. public debate as personal attack, raising question as personal challenge, voting openly as public pressure on individuals, eye-contact as showing personal anger/threat, etc. On the other hand, they convert/interpret everything into personal matters: e.g. gifts and favours are ways and means to cultivate and reinforce relations, decision is to be made by consensus of persons who are willing to give up personal interest/opinion for the sake of the solidarity of the group.

Appointment/promotion to desirable positions is not based on objective criteria or institutional rule but personal preference based on relationship. They see no wrong in "patronage" appointment and no need for "conflict of interest" guideline. The relational network is more important than personal performance/productivity or planned program (e.g. church planting). Of course, the ethnic worker will not tell this to the NAC's face; after all there is no personal bond or relational base to enable him to do so. (see **Table 3** below).

Table 3 - THINGS RELATED TO PROCESS

AREA	CAUCASIAN *CONCEPTION/ PERCEPTION/ OPERATION*	NON-CAUCASIAN *FASCINATION/FRUSTRATION*
SELF	independent & autonomous	"the Caucasian 'self' is fascinating from distance but fearful when near"
	"us" defined by association of personal choice based on interest & achievement	"us" defined by involuntary grouping, e.g. family, gender, etc.
OPERARTION	task-oriented	"too much concern for efficiency will turn you into an impersonal bureaucrat"
	means-oriented	"that's dehumanizing"
	effort-optimism: "if there is a will; there is a way"	relation-optimism: "if you have the right relation/connection; there is a way." There is an obsession for harmony & honor.
	prefer change (future = bright & progressive)	"avoid change if at all possible because it is risky" (future = uncertainty & fear)
	time-conscious for punctuality & program	people-conscious for the privileged to ensure the event is good regardless of the time
	analytical/critical understanding will being improvement & progress	relational approach with smooth handling is the way to ensure harmony & peace
INTERACTION	eye-contact: = honesty & sincerity	avoid eye-contact to show respect; especially when addressing members of the opposite sex
	objective social interaction	"how dare you attack my idea & oppose me"
	church planting: budget, planning & program	"start nothing unless the right persons & the right network are in place"
	"gift-giving to leader in high position is bribery"	"gifts & favors are necessary to reinforce relationship"
	decision-making: counting votes of individuals	"a leader should be able to read the general sentiment of the group & nurture consensus"
	conflict resolution: by confrontation & direct settlement	avoid conflict at all cost; otherwise use subtle communication & mediator

Conclusion

There are many positive examples of successful cooperation between ethnic workers and NACs. There are more reasons for better cooperation among Christians of different ethnic backgrounds: "one body...one hope, one Lord, one faith..." and we are "to strive to maintain the unity..." (Eph 4:1-7). We just have to be ethnically better informed, culturally more sensitive, ministerially more cooperative to show the world the true color of our love for one another (John 13:34-35) regardless of the color of our skin or the label of our denominations.

Appendix - INTERCULTURAL MINISTRIES QUESTIONNAIRE

> The following TOPICS and SUB-TOPICS are provided to trigger your thoughts on various aspects of church planting and pastoral ministries among ethnic groups. The list is not at all exhaustive. Feel free to express your experiences and views on whichever is applicable to you. Use extra paper if you need to. Your input on any or all of this is very important. THANK YOU!!

AWARENESS (cultural, denominational, personal struggles, etc.)

EXPECTATIONS (denominational, family, personal, energy level, ministry time, productivity, success, etc.)

FACILITIES (community center, home, office, worship center, etc.)

FINANCES (ministry expenses, rental, personal salary, etc.)

DENOMINATION (attitudes, communication, collegial feedback, fairness, freedom, supervision, leadership style, polity support, time line for growth, etc.)

LEADERSHIP (clergy, layperson, maturity, personal, style, etc.)

PREPARATION (community research, ministerial training, etc.)

STRATEGY/METHODS (creativity, denominational, personal, etc.)

SUPPORT (colleagues in ministry, family, financial, moral, personnel, struggles or crises, etc.)

SUPERVISION (degree of, frequency, quality, written report, etc.)

RESOURCES (advertising, evangelistic tracts, finances, stationery media, nurturing materials, personnel, business cards, etc.)

Before I started this ministry I wish somebody had told me the following:

The challenges/barriers/problems in intercultural ministries are:

The discouragements in intercultural ministries are:

The joys/rewards of intercultural ministries are:

Other comments (if any):

END NOTES:

[1] T.V. Thomas, born in Malaysia of Indian descent, is the International Minister-at-Large for Every Home International/Canada and Director of the Centre for Evangelism and World Mission in Regina, Saskatchewan, Canada. Dr. Thomas has had Christian services in Malaysia, India, U.S.A. and Canada in student ministry, evangelism, teaching, and administration. He was the former Professor of the Murray W. Downey Chair of Evangelism, Canadian Bible College/Canadian Theological Seminary.

[2] Enoch Wan, born in China educated in Hong Kong and the U.S.A., is the Professor of Missions and Anthropology and the Director of the Doctor of Missiology Program at the Reformed Theological Seminary in Jackson, MS. He has had Christian services in the capacity of pastoral/church planting (in Hong Kong, New York, Vancouver, Toronto), missionary (in Australia, the Philippines, Venezuela), and seminary teaching (in Hong Kong, Canada and the U.S.A.). He also served on the national Board of Directors of the C. & M. A. Canada for two-terms (eight years) and the national Canadian Chinese Alliance Churches Executive Committee for about ten years.

[3] Ethnography is a descriptive study of a particular culture.

[4] Social scientist such as Kenneth Pike and James Spradley use the "emic" (insider's perspective) as compared to the "etic" (outsider's perspective) in research strategy. The presenters are both of non-Caucasian background with first-hand experience personally and have gathered inputs from ethnic co-workers in the survey study.

Chapter 14

ETHNIC RECEPTIVITY AND INTERCULTURAL MINISTRIES[1]

ENOCH WAN

For past decades Canada had a leading role in sending missionaries into many countries of the world. Then came the 1980's, and many of those countries closed their doors to outside messengers (although Brother Andrew has maintained that there is no country you can't get into - just ones you can't get out of). Just when we are lamenting these hindrances, God seemed to be opening a new door of opportunity. Canada was inviting record numbers of immigrants to join us, many from countries which were closed to our missionaries.

We are now confronting a new mission field, yet in some ways are unequipped for facing this challenge. Donald McGavran has given us the necessary descriptive terms: "E-1 evangelism," meaning that which reaches our own kind of people; "E-2 evangelism," which requires crossing some kind of barrier, usually physical, such as going into a new community; and "E-3 evangelism," which crosses cultural and language barriers as well as physical barriers, such as going to a new country. He says, "for E-3 evangelism, the church must have a corps of missionaries with special training." While we have trained our "foreign missionaries for crossing these barriers and are putting forth a great effort, particularly in Vision 2000, to equip for E-1 evangelism, what may be lacking is help for E-2 evangelism reaching these new Canadians who are physically close yet culturally distant.

Most of us would recognize that there needs to be a difference in strategy between E-1, E-2, and E-3 evangelism. But as we confront the E-2 sphere of evangelism, is there anything that can help us to better relate the gospel? When we send our missionaries to other lands, we train them to look for ways that God has prepared that culture for the gospel, ways to look for receptivity that will affect strategy. We need to do the same as we look at reaching these new cultures coming to our land. In fact, our strategy for evangelism will be deficient if this "cultural integration/variation" is not taken into consideration. There are factors of integration and receptivity that can help us better communicate the gospel to that culture.

In this chapter, we will look at informative cases or situations for contextualized evangelism of different ethnic groups, followed by the interpretive analysis of cultural integration/variation factors and concluded by instructive suggestions for our evangelism and church-planting strategies within these new Canadian cultures.

Informative Understanding of Cultural Integration/Variation:

Our mandate is clear. The church is to evangelize the nations or the people-groups (Mt 24:14; 28:19). Like the Christ Incarnate who in order to reach, men became a man, and lived among the Aramaic-speaking Jews in the context of Greco-Roman culture, Christians are to evangelize different people-groups within the context of their cultures, which is "contextualized evangelism."

The general pattern of evangelization practiced by Anglophone Caucasian Christians needs to be contextualized when evangelizing other ethnic groups and modified according to their various degree of cultural integration/variation. Several simple but informative studies of contextualized evangelism will be presented to help us understand how this can be applied to various ethnic groups.

Means of Pre-evangelism

One of the characteristics of contemporary Canadian culture is the "impersonal informational" aspect. This may be the cumulative effects of industrialization, urbanization, technological revolution and information explosion, etc. consequently, the kind of pre-evangelism efforts that evangelicals use extensively involve mass media (e.g. telephone, radio, television, printed literature and published magazine). These are exclusively in English, predominantly informational, and very impersonal.

The usual means of pre-evangelism by anglophone Caucasian Christians are inadequate and inefficient in reaching new immigrants who are functionally illiterate in English, relatively untouched by the mass media, and socially isolated from the anglophone Caucasian Christians' social network (typically of middle-class, professional, suburban dwellers). Canadians of South Asian origin (mostly English-speaking, relatively more westernized professionals) may be touched by the impersonal-informational means of pre-evangelism. However, most Canadians who came as refugees (Vietnamese, Hispanic or Arab origin) are non-English speaking, non-professional immigrants. This group of Canadians will not be touched by the typical means of impersonal-informational pre-evangelism by anglophone Caucasian Christians.

Method of Contact

First generation immigrants are culturally less integrated into the mainstream of anglophone Caucasians culture than their local born descendants. They usually have frequent social interaction with their own people (i.e. extended family and kindred spirits) in their native tongues. Newspapers, videos and movies which are printed or produced in their native languages are the main media of communication and the sources of information. Being proportionately small in number, their social relationships are more personal and intimate. Thus, pre-evangelism is best done through personal contacts and private interaction, which better demonstrates the virtue of a Christlike character than extensive reliance on mass media.

Message of the Gospel

Western culture has a Greco-Roman, politico-legal base and Judeo-Christian ethical foundation. The Greek social system of city-state, the Roman law, etc. have been well-developed for "millennia" in the West. The influence of the Judeo-Christian value system and moral code has left its mark in the mind and heart of people in the context of western civilization, so much so that anthropologists who have conducted cross-cultural comparative studies have classified the western culture as a "guilt culture" in contrast to the "shame culture" of the East (e.g. Japanese, Chinese, Vietnamese, etc.).

The Protestant reformation had a strong emphasis on the doctrine of "justification by faith." The favorite New Testament books of western evangelicals for reading and preaching are usually Romans and Galatians. Anglophone Caucasian Christians usually define "sinners" as "people violating God's law" and the message of salvation is expressed in terms of "forgiveness of sin...the penal substitution of Christ...imputed righteousness." The gospel is introduced in the form of "law-principle," and in terms of "justification by faith in Christ as Saviour."

Message in Culture

People of the East give a high priority to "honour" and avoid "shame" at all cost. For example, a Japanese would rather die than live in disgrace. To him wealth or health is dispensable and deniable in order to avoid shame or acquire fame. This is in contrast to the life-long quest for success as defined by material gain of the capitalist, entrepreneur in the West. Easterners, such as Japanese, Koreans, Chinese, Vietnamese, Indians, can better grasp the shameful state and severed relationship between God and man (Gen. 9:1-11. 22), man and woman which was due to the fall (Gen. 3:16), and the need for salvation. They will be more willing to accept Christ as the "Blame bearer" (Gen. 3:7-8; Mk. 16:34), the mediator-reconciliator (Rom 5; 2 Cor. 5; Eph. 2; Heb. 9) for sinners who suffer because of severed relationship and the subsequent shameful state. If the message of the gospel, presented to relational people of the "shame culture," was in terms of personal "reconciliation" instead of justification (as in the farm of the "Four Spiritual Laws"), it will be better understood and more gratefully received.

Of course, the "whole counsel of God" (Act 20:27) should be taught eventually in a discipleship program. But nobody should be alienated from the Kingdom of God because they are culturally unable to grasp the overemphasized "forensic" aspect of the gospel and therefore, unprepared to accept the "penal substitution of Christ" as presented by anglophone Caucasian Christians in evangelism.

Message of Power

Most non-Caucasian Canadians from the third-world take the spirit world very seriously. The presence and power of evil forces and demonic beings are readily recognized. Many have witnessed demonic manifestations or even personally experienced demonic oppression or possession. Their superstition and fear of the spirits would have prepared them to receive the "good news' of a mighty but merciful Christ. The classical Christian view of Christ's death and atonement (Col. 2; Heb. 2), setting us free from evil power, would be better appreciated than the rational, logical argument of the existence of God. They want to embrace Christ and experience His victory and love that could set them free from fear and fate (1 John 3:8; 4:4,18; 5:4- 6, 18-20).

The primary message of the gospel for these ethnic Canadians is not a hope to enter heaven "by and by" and deliverance from hell in the afterlife. They want to experience the deliverance from curse, fate, fear, etc. in the "here and now." To these ethnic Canadians, the freedom and joy in Christ is a liberating message and life style. It is something that can be declared clearly, demonstrated powerfully and experienced daily.

Method of Evangelism

In the context of western culture (anglophone Caucasians of Canada, U.S.A., and Europe), the most popular and commonly used method of evangelism had been the well publicized mass rally. Ideally, it is a well organized operation, meeting in a public place (church building, public hall or arena), and featuring excellent programs. People are encouraged to make a personal decision and public profession of faith by raising their hand or coming forward.

This has been a very effective method of evangelism to reach anglophone Caucasians who are relatively more individualistic in decision-making, more public in religious expression and more program oriented in their social gathering.

Method of Deciding

Most ethnics of non-western origin are not individualistic (self-directed) in their decision-making process. Whether it be Canadian Natives, East Indian Immigrants, Chinese, et cetera, they are more communal (family, clan-centered called "other-directed") in social behavior, including decision-making. Their social gathering is usually more event, people-oriented (not program-oriented or time-conscious). They wait till the people are there, even though it be "late" in time according to Caucasian standard.

Among many ethnic groups (e,g. Japanese, Chinese, East Indian, Africans, Hispanics, Moslems, Sikhs), children, wives, and unmarried young adults are to submit to the authority and ruling of their parents, husbands and the elderly males. Unlike anglophone Caucasians, religious resolution (including acceptance of Christ as Savior) is to many of them a private family matter. The general pattern of anglophone Caucasians in thinking like public confession of faith, or making an instantaneous and personal decision, needs some rethinking before imposing it on the new converts of different ethnic origins.

Meaning of Grace

When evangelizing, ethnic Canadian evangelicals should modify their "felt need" approach of outreach often used with anglophone Caucasians. Many times we give the promise of prosperity and problem solving, or the Gospel of health and wealth, success and happiness. We parade the newly converted movie star, the professional athlete or the successful businessman in our evangelistic rallies, and in their stage show type of program, we call for a simplistic or emotional "acceptance of Christ."

The problem is that it gives ethnic Canadians the idea of "cheap grace" and of superficial showmanship to the gospel. Many ethnic Canadians from Buddhist, Hindu, and Islam backgrounds take pride in their religious devotion, personal discipline, and ascetic deliberation of their ancestral faith. They despise and decline easy religious experiences as too shallow, superficial and simplistic. In fact, many of them will have to pay a high cost for the change of allegiance to the Lordship of Christ but would be willing to do so for the One who paid a costly price for their salvation (Eph. 1:17; 1Cor. 8:19-20).

An extensive period of in-depth follow-up of these ethnic converts is necessary to deal with problems such as family opposition, carry over superstition and syncretism, social ostracism, lingering demonic entanglement, et cetera. The cost of discipleship (Mt 16:24; Lk. 14:25-35), personally and socially, as part of a well developed evangelism program, is not to be underestimated. The fast-food mentality and quick-fix methodology of anglophone Caucasians should not be assumed as valid when evangelizing ethnic Canadians.

These factors were meant to inform as to the importance of "contextualized evangelism" among anglo-phone non-Caucasian Canadians. We now need to interpret some of the cultural "integration/variation factors" that can help us in our evangelism and church planting.

Interpretive View of Cultural Integration/Variation

Canada, like the U.S.A., is an immigrant country. All Canadians, except the Canadian Indians, are either overseas-born immigrants or local born offsprings. However, there is a dominant anglophone Caucasian culture (or "host culture") by virtue of its population size and duration of tradition. Although Canada is a bilingual nation, it has a multi-cultural population. There are many ethnic groups (East Indian, Chinese, Ukrainian, Italian) maintaining their subcultures in the cultural mosaic of Canada. The trend toward racial divergence and cultural variation in Canada is a fact reflected in the immigration policy of recent years.

The "host culture" of Canadian anglophone Caucasians is a mixture of many cultures, such as British, Scottish, Irish, American, and yet is different from the origin of each. For example, anglophone Caucasians usually have morning breakfast, noon lunch and evening dinner (with snacks or coffee breaks in between) in contrast to that of the British having morning breakfast, noon "dinner", afternoon "tea" and night supper. Though there be regional variations, this is a distinctive of the "host culture" of anglophone Caucasian

Canadians. Both the non-English speaking, overseas-born-ethnic ("OBE") and the local-born ethnic ("LBE") will be gradually integrated into this "host culture."

There are many factors contributing to the rate and extent of the cultural integration of ethnic Canadians. Among them are English language skills, level of education, type of occupation, residential pattern, place of birth, duration of stay, etc. detailed discussion of these factors is beyond the scope of this chapter but two dimensions affecting cultural integration/variation are included in the following discussion.

The two major dimensions in the process of cultural integration are: objective predisposition ("the degree of resemblance of an OBE/LBE's own culture to the host culture"), and the subjective preference ("an OBE/LBE's personal choice in terms of motivation, emotion and volition towards cultural integration). These two can also be the deterrent factors against varying degrees (in intensity and extensiveness) of cultural integration with resultant cultural variation. (see the A---B scale in **Figure #1**.)

Figure 1 - CULTURAL INTEGRATION/VARIATION & READINESS SCALE

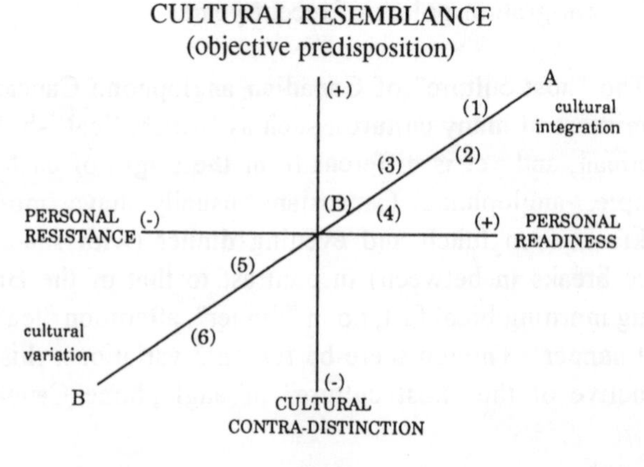

NOTES:

1. OBE Canadian from the Philippines
2. OBE Canadian from Pakistan
3. LBE Canadian of East Indian parents
4. OBE Canadian from India
5. LBE Canadian Vitnanese (Buddhist from the countryside)
6. OBE Canadian Vitnamese (Atheist from Bangkok)

(B) point of "acculturation" (see footnote 3)

For example, a Canadian Filipino (1 in **Figure #1**) comes from a cultural background with several centuries of Spanish colonization and decades of American domination. He, as compared to a Moslem from Pakistan (2 in **Figure #1**); can be culturally integrated into the "host culture" easier than the latter. The cultural resemblance of (1) to the "host culture," contrasting to the culture contra-distinction of (2) from the "host culture," would make shift of (1) to the "host culture" smoother and faster than that of (2).

On the other hand, though (3) and (4) are both from India, the lack of personal readiness of OBE (4) will restart the process of cultural integration as compared to LBE-(3) who has been born and raised in Canada. The ethnic background of (5) and (6) is Vietnamese, yet LBE-(5) has less cultural and religious barrier to overcome than OBE-(6); the latter most likely will prefer and remain to be more Vietnamese than the former.

This simple but basic understanding of cultural integration and variation provides the basis of the following discussion on evangelism and discipleship.

Integration/Variation re: Evangelism and Discipleship

If an OBE/LBE's cultural background is more integrated with or similar to the "host culture," then generally there is more opportunity for him or her to hear the gospel and more flexibility for that person to enjoy the freedom of accepting Christ. This leads us to a brief discussion of the two major dimensions of both the Christian's conversion and maturity and the evangelization of non-Christians. (C--D of **Figure #2** is an evangelism-discipleship scale).

For example, if all things are equal, a new convert to Christianity will grow to maturity faster and stronger (1 in **Figure #2**) if he experiences favorable circumstances and has a teachable spirit. If an individual (6 in **Figure #2**) does not objectively have the opportunity to hear the gospel and the freedom to accept Christ, nor does he personally show a willingness to embrace the Christian faith, he will not likely become a Christian. In fact, he might be strongly resistant to the gospel.

The following diagram illustrates the somewhat obvious, if both (2a) and (2b) of **Figure #2** are born-again Christians with the same kind of teachable spirit, (2a) being from a Christian home will be easier to disciple than (2b) being from a Moslem home. Both (3a) and (3b) are born again Christians Catholic Filipino homes, (3a) with a teachable spirit will mature spiritually easier and faster than (3b) who is not receptive to spiritual things. Given that both (4a) and (4b) are unsaved and unchurched, if (4a) has less opportunity to hear the gospel and has to face strong opposition from Sikh parents, then he usually will be more difficult to be evangelized than (4b). If both (5) and (6) are non-Christian immigrants from Singapore, the churchgoing and less resistant (5) will more likely be reached by the gospel than unchurched and resistant person like (6).

Figure 2 - THE CULTURAL INTEGRATION AND SPIRITUAL FORMATION (EVANGELISM & DISCIPLESHIP) SCALE

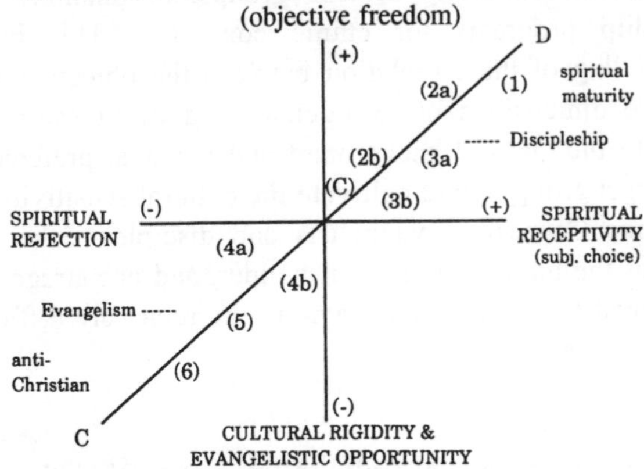

NOTES:

1. mature Christian (from Christian home, with teachable spirit)
2a. born-again Christian (from Christian home)
2b. born-again Christian (from Moslem home)
3a. born-again Christian (from Filipino home, with teachable spirit)
3b. born-again Christian (from Filipino home, without teachable spirit)
4a. unsaved, unchurched (of Sikh parents)
4b. unsaved, unchurched (of Catholic parents)
5. unsaved, Canadian from Singapore (churchgoing, mildly resistant to the Gospel)
6. unsaved, Canadian from Singapore (unchurched, strongly resistant to the Gospel)
C. point of conversion

The cultural integration/variation and spiritual formation (evangelism and discipleship) scale presented above is a useful conceptual tool for developing evangelism strategies to reach different ethnic Canadians, evaluating evangelistic efforts among culturally diverse groups, or planning for discipleship programs for ethnic converts. This basic understanding of the correlation between the objective and subjective dimensions of evangelism and discipleship (in relation to the cultural background and personal preference of the target group) could cultivate the cultural sensitivity of anglophone Caucasian evangelists and disciples, calm the anxiety of the hard-working soul winner, and encourage the disheartened Christian worker among the relatively difficult ethnic Canadians.

Instructive Suggestions of Cultural Integration/Variation for Church Planting

Local churches differ from one another in shape, size, polity, language, race, etc. Of these many different factors, the following discussion will deal with only ethnic diversity and congregational preference (in terms of cultural integration/variation).

After conducting successful evangelization and developing good discipleship programs among ethnic Canadians, a church planter (or the founding ethnic members) will have the option of forming a church that is not necessarily homogeneous or heterogeneous but somewhere on the continuum between the two. In other words, it may be a single-congregation of a homogeneous group, but there are options of being a single-congregation with subgroups making it a multi-congregation church as shown in the E---F scale of **Figure #3**.

Figure #3 - THE CONGREGATION TYPE AND CHURCH PLANTER'S OPTION SCALE

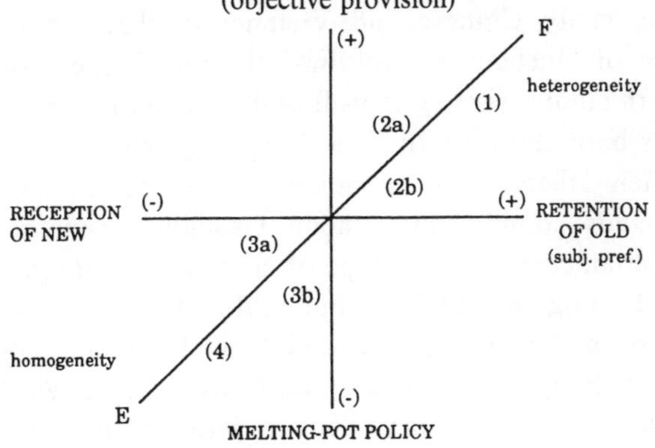

NOTES:

1. heterogeneous & multi-congregation church
2a. multilingual & multicultural church
2b. bilingual & bicultural church
3a. monolingual & monocultural church, ethnic but open (OBE + LBE + etc.)
3b. monolingual & bicultural church, ethnic but conservative (OBE dominant)
4. monolingual & heterogeneous church (only OBE or LBE)

It is natural and logical, and even expedient for ethnic Canadians to form a monolingual and homogeneous church as in example (4) in **Figure #3**. This is a common practice of OBE Canadian Christians, particularly seen in all early Mennonite churches. The opposite alternative is to form a multilingual, heterogeneous and multi-congregational church (i.e., 1 in **Figure #3**).

The operation of a multilingual and multicultural church (2a of **Figure #3**) would usually require a lot of mutual respect, careful coordination and Christian love to ensure the health and well-being of such a heterogeneous church. For example, many Chinese and Vietnamese churches in the province of Quebec are multilingual using French for the local born ethnics (LBE), as well as the mother tongue of the overseas born ethnics (OBE), and also English.

Often there are members from several ethnic backgrounds joining anglophone Caucasian churches in metropolitan centers. This type of church (2b of **Figure #3**) is usually English speaking but multicultural. This is a version of the "international church" found in major cities in the world (Bangkok, Manila, Hong Kong, Mexico, etc.).

Ethnic churches may begin with a monolingual immigrant congregation made up of OBEs. Later, when the new generation(s) of LBE or new converts from other ethnic backgrounds increase in number, the church may remain monolingual (of the mother tongue of OBE) yet become multicultural (3a of **Figure #3**).

The more conservative ethnic church dominated by OBE (without integrating other ethnic Canadians or accommodating the LBE) may remain monolingual (mother tongue of OBE) but bicultural (3b) of **Figure #3**.

In a pluralistic and multicultural society like Canada (and the U.S.A.. in contrast. for example, to many Moslem countries), the E-F scale is a continuum of heterogeneity and homogeneity with many options for church planting. This is a good and healthy model especially when the population of Canada and the United States is changing towards greater racial diversity and cultural plurality.

Conclusion

Cultural integration/variation is an interesting and important aspect of Canadian life. Those who are committed to evangelism and church planting in Canada must take into consideration the multi-ethnic, multi-cultural trend of the population. The vision of the lostness of man and the mission of nationwide and world-wide evangelization require new efforts and cooperation on the part of Canadian Christians (anglophone Caucasians, overseas-born ethnics and local-born ethnics alike) to share the gospel with the unsaved and unchurched, whatever their race may be. And as we are willing to be His witnesses, He has promised the power of the Holy Spirit, not only in our Jerusalem (E-1) or just to the far corners of the earth (E-3), but also in our "E-2 evangelism" -- our Canadian "Judea and Samaria."

---

[1] Reprinted with permission of Church Leadership Library from *Reclaiming a Nation*, edited by Arnell Motz, 1990.

EPILOGUE

Don Moore
Executive Director - Vision 2000 Canada

"I believe it is now time for third world countries to send missionaries to Canada," I recall declaring at a private dinner with the leaders from 20 nations during the Lausanne II Consultation on World Evangelization in Manila, Philippines. Through our Vision 2000 Canada research, I have come to the realization that Canada is gradually losing its historic and significant influence in global missions. In fact, the influence and size of our evangelical community in Canada is clearly declining.

During that same dinner, I went on to use the influx of Filipino immigrants to Canada as an illustration of the tremendous need for evangelism and church planting. This is why I consider this collection of papers as vitally important if we are going to understand and tackle the tremendous challenges in reaching our ethnic communities.

With a rapidly growing awareness of the ethnic communities that are growing in our urban centres, it is time we recognize our responsibilities, repent of our wrong attitudes and actions, and reevaluate the relationships that we as individuals and congregations have with our new ethnic neighbours.

As God's people, we have the responsibility to provide every person in Canada, including our ethnics, the opportunity to see, hear and respond to the gospel by the year 2000. Unfortunately, many churches are so totally consumed with their internal "family matters" and maintenance that to be mission-minded beyond the walls of the church towards caucasians, let alone ethnics, is highly unlikely. It is time we seek God's face (II Chron 7:14) for a fresh vision of how we can best fulfil our responsibilities to the "Great Commission" lest our ethnic communities become known as our "Great Omission."

In seeking God's face, I am convinced that many of us will have to repent of attitudes and actions that have simply not been Christ-like towards our ethnic communities. Recently, I learned of a congregation who passed a motion confirming their commitment to remain a caucasian church, encouraging those in the neighbouring ethnic communities to worship elsewhere. It is time for reconciliation to take place and for us to repent, whether it be for neglect or intentional isolation.

This tangible evidence of repentance and reconciliation would result in love and unity, which I know would speak volumes to a society that is wrestling to integrate these same communities. The consultation, **MISSIONS WITHIN REACH**, from which this compendium resulted, is an excellent example of what needs to be expanded and even more highly profiled as we seek to reach our nation with the gospel. It is time for us, through dialogue and action, to creatively explore together how to nurture growing relationships between all peoples of Canada.

RESOURCE LIST

Anderson, Leith. 1992. A Church of the 21st Century. Minneapolis, MN: Bethany House Publishers.

Appleby, Jerry L. 1986. Missions Have Come Home to America. Kansas City, MO: Beacon Hill Press.

Arbuckle, Gerald A. 1990. Earthing the Gospel: An Inculturation Handbook for the Pastoral Worker. Maryknoll, NY: Orbis Books.

Bibby, Raginald W. 1987. Fragmented Gods: The Poverty and Potential of Religion in Canada. Toronto, ON: Irwin Publishing.

Bibby, Reginald W. 1993. Mosaic Madness: The Poverty and Potential of Life in Canada. Toronto, ON: Stoddart Publishing Co.

Bienvenue, Rita M. and Goldstein, Jay E. 1985. Ethnicity and Ethnic Relations in Canada. Second Edition. Toronto: Butterworth & Co.

Bolaria, B. Singh, and Li, Peter S. 1985. Racial Oppression in Canada. Toronto: Garamond Press.

Bush, Luis and Lutz, Lorry. 1990. Partnering in Ministry: The Direction of World Evangelism. Downers Grove, IL: InterVarsity Press.

Crysdale, Stewart and Wheatcroft, Les, eds. 1976. Religion in Canadian Society. Toronto: The Macmillan Company of Canada.

Dion, L. 1989. <u>Quebec 1945-2000</u>. Tome I. Quebec: PUL.
Dodd, Carley H. and Fontalvo, Frank F., eds. 1987. <u>Intercultural Skills for Multicultural Societies</u>. Washington, DC: SIETAR International.

Elliott, Jean Leonard, ed. 1971. <u>Native Peoples</u>. Scarborough, Ontario: Prentice-Hall of Canada.

Ford, Leighton. 1994. <u>The Power of Story: Rediscovering the Oldest, Most Natural Way to Reach People for Christ</u>. Colorado Springs, CO: NavPress.

George, Carl F. 1991. <u>Prepare Your Church for the Future</u> Tarrytown, NY: Fleming H. Revell Co.

Goldberg, M.A. and Mercer, J. 1989. <u>The Myth of the North American City</u>. Vancouver, BC: University of British Columbia.

Harrison, Daniel, and Aeshliman, Gordon. 1985. <u>Romancing the Globe</u>. Markham, ON: InterVarsity Press.

Hesselgrave, David. 1989. <u>Planting Churches Cross-Culturally</u>. Grand Rapids: Baker Book House.

Hofstede, Geert. 1984. <u>Culture's Consequences: International Differences in Work-related Values</u>. Beverly Hills, CA: SAGE Publications, Inc.

Hopler, Thom, and Hopler, Marcia. 1993. <u>Reaching the World Next Door</u>. Downer Grove, IL: InterVarsity Press.

Hunter III, George G. 1992. How to Reach Secular People. Nashville, TN: Abingdon Press.

International Journal of Intercultural Relations. 1986: Vol 10 No. 2. New York: Pergamon Press.

Kalbach, Warren E. 1970. The Impact of Immigration on Canada's Population. Ottawa: Dominion Bureau of Statistics.

Knox, R.H., report director. 1980. Indian Conditions: A Survey. Ottawa: Published under the authority of the Minister of Indian Affairs and Northern Development.

Kohls, L. Robert. 1984. Survival kit for overseas living. Yarmouth, ME: Intercultural Press, Inc.

Krauter, Joseph F. and Davis, Morris. 1978. Minority Canadians: Ethnic Groups. Ontario: Methuen Publications.

Lean, Gart. 1990. Cast Out Your Nets. Ottawa, ON: Grosvenor Books.

Li, Peter S. and Bolaria, B. Singh, eds. 1983. Racial Minorities in Multicultural Canada. Toronto: Garamond Press.

Ligenfelter, Sherwood & Marvin K. Mayers. 1986. Ministering Cross-Culturally. Grand Rapids, MI: Baker Book House.

Lyon, Louise C. and Friesen, John W. 1969. Culture Change and Education: A Study of Indian and Non-Indian Views in Southern Alberta. Calgary: The University of Calgary.

Mann, William E. 1955. Sect, Cult and Church in Alberta. Toronto: University of Toronto Press.

Mohabir, Philip. 1984. Worlds Within Reach - Cross-cultural Witness. Kent, England: Hodder and Stotten Mill Road.

Motz, Arnell, ed. 1990. Reclaiming a Nation, rev. ed. Richmond, BC: Church Leadership Library.

Mullins, Mark. 1989. Religious Minorities in Canada. Queenstown, Ontario: The Edwin Mullen Press.

Padinjarekara, Joseph. 1991. Christ in Ancient Vedas. Burlington, ON: Welch Publishing Co.

Posterski, D. and Barker, Irwin, I. 1993. Where's a Good Church? Winfield, BC: Wood Lake Books Inc.

Posterski, Donald C. 1993. True to You. Winfield, BC: Wood Lake Books Inc.

Pusch, Margaret D., ed. 1979. Multicultural Education: A Cross Cultural Training Approach. Yarmouth, ME: Intercultural Press, Inc.

Raj, Santosh. 1991. Understanding Sikhs And Their Religion. Winnipeg, MB: Kindred Press.

Romano, Dugan. 1988. Inter-Cultural Marriage: Promises & Pitfalls. Yarmouth, ME: Intercultural Press, Inc.

Roxburgh, Alan. 1993. Reaching a New Generation. Downers Grove, IL: InterVarsity Press.

Seelye, H. Ned. 1984. Teaching Culture: Strategies for Intercultural Communication. Lincolnwood, IL: National Textbook Company.

Sikkema, Mildred and Niyekawa, Agnes. 1987. Design for Cross-Cultural Learning. Yarmouth, ME: Intercultural Press, Inc.

Simmons, Tony. 1988. Canadian Ethnic Studies: Book of Readings. Canada: Athabasca University.

Simmons, Tony. 1988. Canadian Ethnic Studies: Study Guide. Canada: Athabasca University.

Singer, Benjamin D. 1972. Communications in Canadian Society. Canada: The Copp Clark Publishing Company.

Slater, Peter. 1977. Religion and Culture in Canada. Canada: Canadian Corporation for Studies in Religion.

Smith, Donald K. 1992. Creating Understanding: A Handbook for Christian Communication Across Cultural Landscapes. Grand Rapids: Zondervan Publishing House.

Smith, Glenn ed. 1992. The Gospel and Urbanization. Montreal: Christian Direction Inc.

Stackhouse, Jr., John. 1985. Canadian Evangelicalism in the Twentieth Century. Toronto: Toronto Press.

Stafford, Tim. 1985. The Friendship Gap - Reaching Out Across Cultures. Markham, ON: InterVarsity Press.

Storti, Craig. 1990. The Art of Crossing Cultures. Yarmouth, ME: Intercultural Press, Inc.

Weeks, William H., Pedersen, Paul B., and Brislin, Richard W., eds. 1989. A Manual of Structured Experiences for Cross-Cultural Learning. Yarmouth, ME: Intercultural Press, Inc.